AF266846

Systematic Theology Workbook for Teens

Guided Questions and Real-Life Application for Christian Living

TABLE OF CONTENTS

INTRODUCTION
START RIGHT HERE

Read and Learn: Why Truth Matters for Your Life Today

You probably have a lot of voices in your ear every day. Your phone buzzes with news and trends. Your friends at school talk about what is right and what is wrong. Your teachers give you facts and theories. Even the music you listen to tells a story about how you should live. All these voices try to tell you what is true. Some people say that truth changes. They say you can have "your truth" and they can have theirs. This makes life feel like you are walking on shifting sand. If everything is true, then nothing is really true. This leaves you feeling lost when life gets hard.

You need a solid place to stand. You need to know what is real and what lasts forever. This is where theology comes in. The word "theology" sounds big and heavy. It sounds like something for old men in dusty libraries. But the word is actually quite simple. It comes from two Greek words: *Theos*, which means God, and *logos*, which means word or study. So, theology is just the study of God. Systematic theology is even simpler. It means we put those truths in order. We look at what the whole Bible says about one topic at a time. We put the pieces of the puzzle together so we can see the big picture.

You are already a theologian. Every time you think about God, you are doing theology. When you wonder why bad things happen, you are doing theology. When you pray for help before a test, you are doing theology. The question is not whether you are a theologian. The question is whether your theology is good or bad. Is it based on your feelings? Is it based on what a famous person said on the internet? Or is it based on what God has actually told us?

Knowing the truth about God changes how you see yourself. It changes how you treat your parents. It changes how you spend your time on a Friday night. God is the creator of everything. He made the stars, the oceans, and your very heart. He is the source of all truth. If we want to know how life works, we have to look at Him. We cannot just guess about God. We cannot make Him up in our own image. We have to see Him as He really is.

Many teens feel like the Bible is just a list of rules. They think God is a judge who waits for them to mess up. But systematic theology shows us a different story. It shows us a God who is holy, yes, but also a God who is full of love. It shows us that God has a plan for history and a plan for you. When you learn these truths, they act like a compass. They point you in the right direction when you feel confused. They give you a reason to hope when things look dark.

This book is a tool for your life. It is not just a textbook for a grade. Each page helps you build a foundation. You will look at what the Bible says about the Word of God, about Jesus, and about the future. You will see how these ideas fit together. Truth is not a cage. It is a key. It sets you free to live the way God meant for you to live.

Why do we need to do this now? Why not wait until you are older? The world wants your mind right now. Advertisements want your money. Apps want your attention. If you do not know what you believe, you will follow whoever speaks the loudest. You will be like a boat without an anchor. A strong faith starts with strong truth. When you know who God is, you can stand firm. You can say "no" to things that hurt you and "yes" to things that bring life.

Think of this workbook as a map. A map does not just tell you where things are. It tells you how to get where you want to go. You want a life that matters. You want a life that feels right and good. That kind of life only comes when you walk with God. To walk with Him, you must know Him. This book will help you do that. We will keep things clear. We will keep things direct. We will focus on the Bible.

Are you ready to build something that lasts? Truth is waiting for you. Let's look at what God has said. Let's see how His words change your world today. This is the start of a new way to see everything.

Apply and Act: Check Your Beliefs and Set Your Goals

This part of the chapter is for you to work through. Grab a pen. Be honest with yourself. There are no wrong answers here, only chances to grow.

1. The Truth Audit

Think about the things you believe right now. Where did those ideas come from? Fill out the table below to see who is influencing your thoughts about God and life.

Topic	What do I believe about this?	Where did I learn this?
Who is God?		
Why am I here?		
What is sin?		
What happens after death?		

Is the Bible true?		

2. The Anchor Test

When you have a bad day or a big problem, what do you do first? Do you check your phone? Do you talk to a friend? Do you pray? Write down your "first response" to stress.

My First Response:____

____

Now, ask yourself: Does this response help me find the truth, or does it just help me forget the problem?

3. Setting Your Goals

You are starting a study that covers the main parts of Christian belief. What do you want to get out of this? Pick three goals from the list below or write your own.

- [   ] I want to know why I can trust the Bible.
- [   ] I want to be able to explain my faith to my friends.
- [   ] I want to feel closer to God when I pray.
- [   ] I want to stop feeling confused about what is right and wrong.
- [   ] I want to see how the Bible fits together.
- [   ] Other:

____

____

4. Real-Life Application: The "Social Media" Challenge

Scroll through your favorite social media app for five minutes. Look at the posts, the ads, and the comments.

- List three "truths" the app is trying to tell you (Example: "You need this product to be happy" or "You are not pretty enough").

____

____

____

Next to each one, write one word that describes how that "truth" makes you feel (Example: anxious, jealous, excited).

- Compare these "truths" to what you know about God. Does God say you need that product to be happy? Does He say your worth is based on your looks?

5. Guided Reflection Questions

Answer these questions in one or two sentences. Keep it brief and clear.

- If someone asked you "Who is God?" right now, what would you say?

  ____

  ____

- What is the biggest question you have about the Bible?

  ____

  ____

- Why do you think it is important for a teen to study theology in 2026?

  ____

  ____

6. A Simple Prayer to Start

Theology is not just a head exercise. It is a heart matter. Read this prayer out loud as you start this book:

"Lord, I want to know You as You really are. Please clear my mind of lies. Help me to see the truth in Your Word. Give me the strength to change my life based on what I learn. I give this time to You. Amen."

7. Commitment Check

To get the most value from this workbook, you need to be consistent.

- **When** will you work on this each week? (Example: Tuesday nights at 7:00 PM)

  ____

  ____

- **Where** will you sit so you don't get distracted?

- **Who** can you talk to about what you are learning? (A parent, a youth leader, or a friend)

CHAPTER 1

STUDY THE WORD (BIBLIOLOGY)

Read and Learn: How God Speaks to Us Through the Bible

If you want to know a person, you have to listen to them talk. You cannot just guess what your best friend thinks about a movie. You have to ask them. You cannot assume your coach is happy with your performance. You have to hear their feedback. The same is true with God. We cannot just look at the clouds and guess what God wants from us. We cannot look at a sunset and know how to get to heaven. Those things show us that God is big and strong. But they do not tell us His name. They do not tell us His plan. For that, we need His words.

Theology starts with a big idea: God spoke. He did not leave us in the dark. He chose to tell us who He is. We call this "revelation." It simply means that God pulled back the curtain. He showed us things we could never find on our own. The main way He does this is through the Bible. This is why we start our study here. If we cannot trust the Bible, we cannot trust anything else we learn about God. The Bible is the foundation for every other truth in this book.

You might hear people say the Bible is just a collection of old stories. They might say it was written by men who lived in tents thousands of years ago. In one way, they are right. Men did write the words down. But there is more to the story. The Bible tells us that "all Scripture is breathed out by God." This comes from 2 Timothy 3:16. Think about that for a second. When you speak, you use your breath. God "breathed" His truth into the minds of the writers. We call this "inspiration."

Inspiration does not mean the writers were like robots. God did not take over their hands and force them to write. Instead, He used their personalities. He used their life experiences. Peter sounds like a fisherman because he was one. Paul sounds like a lawyer because he was trained like one. Yet, every word they wrote was exactly what God wanted said. This is a miracle. It means the Bible is 100% the work of men and 100% the work of God.

Because God is the true author, the Bible has a special quality. It is "inerrant." This is a fancy way of saying it does not have any errors. God does not lie. God does not make mistakes. If the Bible is God's Word, then the Bible must be true in everything it says. It is true when it talks about history. It is true when it talks about science. Most importantly, it is true when it talks about how you can be saved. You can trust it more than you trust your own feelings. Feelings change every day. The Word of God stays the same.

The Bible is also "sufficient." This means it gives us everything we need to know God and follow Him. You do not need a secret code to find God. You do not need a new vision or a special dream. God has already said what He needs to say in the 66 books of the Bible. It is a complete map for your life. It tells you where you came from. It tells you why the world is broken. It tells you how Jesus fixes that brokenness.

Lastly, the Bible has "authority." Since God is the King of the universe, His words are the final law. When the Bible says something is wrong, it is wrong. When it says something is good, it is good. We do not get to pick and choose the parts we like. We do not get to cut out the verses that make us feel uncomfortable. Following the Bible means we put God in the driver's seat. We let Him set the rules for our relationships, our money, and our time.

Reading the Bible is not just about gaining facts. It is about meeting a Person. When you open your Bible, you are sitting down to listen to the Creator of the stars. He wants to talk to you. He wants to guide you. But you have to show up. You have to read. You have to listen. This chapter will help you see how to do that well. It will show you how the Bible is organized. It will help you see why it is the most important book you will ever own.

The world will tell you that the Bible is outdated. People will say it does not fit with modern life. Do not believe them. The grass withers and the flowers fall, but the Word of our God stands forever. This is the only book that can truly change your heart. It is the only book that offers real hope. Let's look at how we can study it and live it out.

Apply and Act: Use a Study Plan and Verify Bible Facts

This section is your chance to put what you just read into practice. Use these exercises to build your confidence in the Word of God.

1. The Structure of the Book

The Bible is one big story, but it is made of many smaller parts. Test your knowledge by filling in the blanks below.

- The Bible has _________ total books.
- There are ________ books in the Old Testament.
- There are ________ books in the New Testament.
- The Bible was written by about ________ different authors.
- It was written over a period of about ________ years.

2. Inspiration vs. Human Ideas

Read 2 Peter 1:20-21. In your own words, explain how a human author wrote a book that actually came from God.

----

3. The "Inerrancy" Case Study

Imagine a friend at school says, "The Bible was written by people, and people make mistakes. So, the Bible must have mistakes too." Based on what you learned in the "Read and Learn" section, how would you answer them? (Hint: Think about who was guiding the authors).

----

4. Bible Fact Check

Pick one of the following verses. Look it up in your Bible and answer the questions below.

Options: Psalm 119:105, Hebrews 4:12, or John 17:17.

- **Verse Reference:**

- **What does this verse say about the Word of God?**

- **How can you apply this verse to a problem you are facing today?**

    ----

5. Practice the "COMA" Method

When you read the Bible, it helps to have a system. Use the **COMA** method on **John 1:1-5**.

- **C - Context:** Who wrote this? Who was it written to? (A quick look at the intro to John in your Bible can help).

- **O - Observation:** What is happening in these verses? What words are repeated?

____

____

- **M - Meaning:** What is the main point the author is trying to make about Jesus (the Word)?

____

____

- **A - Application:** How does knowing that Jesus is "the Word" change how you think about God?

____

____

6. Real-Life Application: The Authority Test

Think about a popular opinion in our culture today (Example: "You should always do what makes you happy").

- **The Opinion:**

____

____

- **What does the Bible say about this?** (Look for a verse about following God's will instead of our own).

____

____

- **Which authority will you follow? Why?**

____

____

7. A 7-Day Bible Reading Plan

Commit to reading the Word every day for one week. Use the checklist below. Read the passage and write one thing you learned about God from it.

Day	Passage	What I Learned About God
Day 1	Psalm 19	
Day 2	Psalm 119:1-16	
Day 3	2 Timothy 3:10-17	
Day 4	Matthew 4:1-11	
Day 5	Isaiah 40:1-8	
Day 6	Deuteronomy 6:1-9	
Day 7	Revelation 22:18-21	

8. Clear Obstacles

What is the biggest thing that stops you from reading the Bible? Is it being busy? Is it being bored? Is it not knowing where to start?

Write down one specific change you can make this week to overcome that obstacle. (Example: "I will put my phone in another room while I read for ten minutes.")

----

9. Summary Question

If the Bible is God's personal message to you, how should that change the way you look at the book on your nightstand?

----

10. Memory Verse Challenge

Try to memorize **Psalm 119:11** this week: *"I have stored up your word in my heart, that I might not sin against you."* Write the verse here three times to help it stick in your mind:

1. --

2. --

3. --

CHAPTER 2

PRAISE THE FATHER (THEOLOGY PROPER)

Read and Learn: Who God Is and Why He Created You

When you hear the word "God," what comes to your mind? Maybe you think of a bright light in the sky. Maybe you think of a strict judge in a courtroom. Or maybe you think of a kind old man sitting on a cloud. Most people have an image of God, but often that image is wrong. We tend to make God look like us. We think He gets moody or tired or surprised. But God is nothing like a human. He is the Creator, and we are the creation. In this chapter, we look at "Theology Proper." This is just a way of saying we are studying God Himself.

To know God, we have to look at His traits. We call these "attributes." These are the things that are always true about Him. Some of these traits belong to God alone. For example, God is "infinite." This means He has no limits. He has no beginning and no end. He does not need sleep. He never runs out of energy. He does not need anyone to help Him. Before the stars existed, God was there. After the earth is gone, God will still be there. This makes Him different from everything else in the universe. Everything we see has a limit, but God is limitless.

Another trait is that God is "immutable." This means He never changes. Think about how much you change. You grow taller. Your tastes in music change. Your moods go up and down. But God is the same yesterday, today, and forever. His promises do not expire. His love does not fade. His rules do not shift based on what is popular. This is good news. It means you can count on Him. When the world feels like it is spinning out of control, God is the rock that never moves.

God is also "omniscient." This means He knows everything. He knows the number of hairs on your head. He knows what you are going to say before you speak. He knows your secrets and your dreams. You can never hide from Him, but you also never have to explain yourself to Him. He already understands. Along with this, He is "omnipotent," or all-powerful. He created the world with a word. He rules over kings and nations. There is no problem in your life that is too big for Him to handle. Finally, He is "omnipresent." He is everywhere at the same time. You are never alone. Whether you are at school, at home, or in a foreign country, God is right there with you.

These traits show us how big God is. But God is not just a powerful force. He is a Person. The Bible tells us that God is "holy." This means He is perfect. He has no sin. He is completely set apart from evil. Because He is holy, He is also "just." He must punish wrong things. He cannot just look the other way when people get hurt. But the Bible also says that "God is love." His love is not a feeling that comes and goes. It is who He is. He is patient. He is kind. He is merciful. He wants a relationship with you.

The most amazing thing about God is that He is our Father. Jesus told us to pray to "Our Father in heaven." This changes everything. It means the Creator of the galaxy wants you to call Him "Abba." This is a word that shows closeness and trust. A good father protects his children. He provides for them. He listens to them. God is the perfect version of a father. Even if your earthly father is not around or has let you down, your Heavenly Father never will.

Why did this great God create you? He did not create you because He was lonely. He was already happy within Himself. He created you to show off His glory. He made you so you could know Him and enjoy Him forever. When you live for God, you are doing what you were made to do. You are like a lightbulb that has finally been plugged in. You start to shine.

Knowing who God is should lead us to worship. When we see how big He is, we feel small in a good way. We realize that we do not have to carry the weight of the world. God has it. We can stop trying to be in control and let Him lead. We can trade our worry for praise. This week, we will focus on seeing God for who He really is. We will move past our small ideas and look at the Great King.

Apply and Act: Map Out God's Traits and See Them in the World

This workbook section helps you move from knowing facts about God to trusting Him in real life.

1. The Attribute Map

In the boxes below, write down four of God's attributes that you just learned about. Under each one, write one way that specific trait helps you today.

Attribute	How this helps me today
Example: **Immutable**	*I don't have to worry if God is mad at me today, because His love stays the same.*
1.	
2.	
3.	

4.	

2. Word Study: Holy

Read **Isaiah 6:1-5**.

- How did Isaiah feel when he saw the holiness of God?

- Why do you think we sometimes forget that God is holy and perfect?

  ----

3. Case Study: The Midnight Worry

Imagine you are lying in bed at midnight. You are worried about a big test tomorrow. You feel like you are all alone and that nobody understands your stress.

- Which attribute of God (Omniscience, Omnipotence, or Omnipresence) applies to this situation?

- Write a one-sentence prayer using that attribute to calm your heart.

  ----

4. The Creation Scavenger Hunt

God's power and beauty are visible in the world He made. Spend 10 minutes outside or looking out a window. Find three things that show you something about God's character.

- **Thing 1:** ____
  What it shows about God: ___________________________________
- **Thing 2:** ____
  What it shows about God: ___________________________________
- **Thing 3:** ____
  What it shows about God: ___________________________________

5. "Abba" Reflection

Read **Matthew 7:9-11**. Jesus compares God to an earthly father.

- If God is a "good Father" who gives "good gifts," how should that change the way you ask Him for things in prayer?

----

6. Sorting Truth from Lies

Check the boxes next to the statements that are Biblically true about God.

- [   ] God is sometimes surprised by the news.
- [   ] God has always existed.
- [   ] God's love for you depends on how good you are today.
- [   ] God is present even when you feel lonely.
- [   ] God is the same today as He was in the Old Testament.

7. Real-Life Application: The Glory Challenge

We were made to reflect God's glory. This means we should act in a way that makes God look good to others.

- Pick one attribute of God you can reflect this week (Example: God is merciful, so I will be merciful to my sibling).

  My Attribute:

The Plan: What is one specific action you will take to show this trait to someone else?

  ----

8. Guided Reflection Questions

Answer these briefly:

- If God knows everything you do (Omniscience), does that make you feel scared or safe? Why?

- Which attribute of God is the hardest for you to understand?

    ____

    ____

- How does knowing God is "Immutable" (unchanging) help you when your friends or family change?

    ____

    ____

9. The Praise List

Take two minutes to write down as many names or descriptions of God as you can think of (Example: King, Shepherd, Rock, Light).

10. Memory Verse Challenge

Memorize **Psalm 102:27**: *"But you are the same, and your years have no end."* Write it out here and underline the word that describes God's immutability:

11. A Step Toward Trust

What is one thing in your life right now that feels "out of control"?

Write down which of God's attributes gives you peace about this situation.

CHAPTER **3**

WORSHIP THE TRINITY (THE TRINITY)

Read and Learn: How God Lives as Father, Son, and Spirit

The most famous math problem in the Bible is this: $1 + 1 + 1 = 1$. This does not make sense in a school classroom, but it is the truth about who God is. We call this the Trinity. The word "Trinity" is not actually in the Bible, but the idea is on almost every page. It describes a God who is one in essence but three in person. This is the hardest thing for our human brains to grasp. But that is actually a good sign. If we could explain every single thing about God, He would not be much of a God. He is far bigger than our logic.

To start, we must be clear that there is only one God. The Bible is very firm on this. In the Old Testament, the people of Israel said a prayer called the *Shema* every day. It says, "Hear, O Israel: The Lord our

God, the Lord is one." Christians do not believe in three gods. We do not have a "main" god and two "helper" gods. We believe in one God. This one God has existed forever as three distinct Persons: the Father, the Son, and the Holy Spirit.

How can one be three? Think about the way God has revealed Himself in the Bible. At the very beginning, in Genesis 1, God says, "Let **us** make man in **our** image." He did not say "Let me make man in my image." There was a conversation happening within God before time began. We see this even more clearly when Jesus is baptized in the Jordan River. The Son is standing in the water. The Holy Spirit descends on Him like a dove. The Father speaks from heaven, saying, "This is my beloved Son." All three Persons are present and active at the same time. They are distinct, but they are not divided.

The three Persons of the Trinity have different roles, but they are all equal in power and glory. The Father is the one who plans and sends. He is the architect of salvation. The Son, Jesus Christ, is the one who obeys the Father and comes to earth. He is the one who died and rose again. The Holy Spirit is the one who applies that work to your life. He lives inside you, teaches you the truth, and gives you strength. They work together in perfect harmony. They never argue. They never have different goals. They are perfectly united in everything they do.

Why does the Trinity matter for your life on a Tuesday afternoon? It matters because God is love. For God to be love before He created humans, He had to have someone to love. Because God is a Trinity, the Father has loved the Son through the Spirit for all eternity. Love is part of who God is, not just something He does. This means that when God loves you, He is inviting you into the same kind of perfect relationship that He has within Himself.

Understanding the Trinity also changes how we pray. We do not just toss words into the air. We pray **to** the Father, **through** the Son, and **by the power of** the Holy Spirit. When you feel like you do not have the right words, the Spirit helps you. When you feel like you are not good enough to talk to God, Jesus stands as your bridge. The Father sits on the throne, ready to listen to His children. The Trinity makes your prayer life possible.

Some people try to explain the Trinity using analogies. They talk about how water can be ice, liquid, or steam. Or they talk about an egg having a shell, a white, and a yolk. These are helpful starts, but they all fall short. Water changes from one form to another, but God never changes. An egg can be broken into parts, but God cannot be divided. It is better to admit that the Trinity is a beautiful mystery. We do not study the Trinity to solve it like a puzzle. We study it so we can worship God for how great He is.

When you think about the Trinity, you should feel a sense of awe. You serve a God who is big enough to create the universe but personal enough to live inside your heart. He is a community within Himself. This shows us that relationships are the most important thing in the world. Since God is a relational Being, you were made for relationship too. You were made to know the Father, love the Son, and walk with the Spirit. This is what it means to be truly alive.

Apply and Act: Find the Trinity in the Bible and in Your Prayers

This section will help you see the Trinity in action and help you think about how this truth changes the way you live.

1. The Trinity Chart

Fill in the chart below to help you remember the distinct roles and the shared nature of the three Persons of God.

Person	His Specific Role	A Verse That Mentions Him
The Father		
The Son		
The Spirit		

2. Scripture Search

Read the following verses and identify which Persons of the Trinity are mentioned in each.

- **Matthew 28:19:**

  ____

  ____

- **2 Corinthians 13:14:**

  ____

  ____

- **1 Peter 1:2:**

  ____

  ____

3. The "Relationship" Reflection

We learned that God is a "community" of three Persons. Because you are made in His image, you are also meant for community.

- Who are three people in your life that help you grow closer to God?

  1. ____

  2. ____

  3. ____

How can you show the kind of unselfish love that exists between the Father, Son, and Spirit to one of these people today?

  ____

  ____

  ____

4. Analogy Alert

As we discussed, most analogies for the Trinity (like the egg or the apple) fail in some way.

- Why is it dangerous to think of God as having "three parts" rather than being "three Persons"?

  ____

  ____

5. Prayer Practice: The Trinitarian Way

Try writing a short prayer below. Be intentional about how you address each Person of the Trinity.

- **Thank the Father** for a specific blessing:

- **Thank the Son** for what He did on the cross:

- **Ask the Spirit** for help with a specific struggle:

----

6. Case Study: The "Three Gods" Question

A friend at school says, "Christians are confusing. You say you believe in one God, but then you talk about Jesus and the Holy Spirit like they are different gods. That's three gods."

- Using what you learned in the "Read and Learn" section, write a 2-sentence response to your friend that is clear and direct.

----

7. Real-Life Application: Worship in Focus

Sometimes we focus so much on Jesus that we forget the Father, or we focus on the Spirit and forget Jesus.

- Which Person of the Trinity do you think about or pray to the most?

- Which Person do you think about the least?

- This week, try to find a worship song that focuses on the Person you think about the least. Write the name of the song here:

----

8. Guided Reflection Questions

Answer these briefly:

- If God were only one Person, could He have been "Love" before He created the world? Why or why not?

- How does it make you feel to know that the Holy Spirit, who is fully God, lives inside you?

- Does the mystery of the Trinity make you want to study the Bible more or less? Why?

  ----

9. The Great Commission Challenge

Read **Matthew 28:18-20**. This is the last thing Jesus said to His followers.

- Why do you think Jesus told them to baptize new believers "in the name" (singular) of the Father, Son, and Holy Spirit?

  ----

10. Truth vs. Error

Read the statements below and mark them as **Truth** or **Error**.

- The Father created the Son a long time ago.   (_______)
- The Spirit is just a force, like electricity.   (_______)
- Jesus is just as much God as the Father is.   (_______)
- God sometimes acts like the Father and sometimes acts like the Son.   (_______)

11. Memory Verse Challenge

Memorize **Numbers 6:24-26**, which is an old blessing that reflects the three-fold nature of God's care. Write it out here:

----

12. The Power of Three

Look at your current life goals. How can you involve the Trinity in them?

- **Father (The Plan):** What do you think God's will is for your future?

- **Son (The Way):** How can you follow Jesus' example in your school or work?

- **Spirit (The Power):** Where do you need the Spirit's strength this week?

  ----

13. Final Thought

If God is a perfect community of love, how should that change the way you deal with people you don't like?

CHAPTER 4

VALUE THE PERSON (ANTHROPOLOGY)

Read and Learn: Why Every Human Has Worth and a Purpose

Who are you? If you ask a scientist, they might say you are a collection of cells and atoms. If you ask a coach, they might say you are a midfielder or a point guard. If you ask an app, you are just a set of data points to be sold to advertisers. Most of the messages you hear every day treat you like a product or a biological accident. They suggest that your value comes from what you can do, how you look, or how much money you will make one day. But the Bible tells a completely different story. It tells us that you are a masterpiece designed by the King of the universe.

The study of humans is called "anthropology." In a Bible study context, we look at what God says about His favorite creation. To find your true identity, you have to go back to the very first page of the Bible. In Genesis 1:26, God says, "Let us make man in our image, after our likeness." This is a huge statement. God did not say this about the mountains. He did not say this about the lions or the stars. He only said it about people. We call this the *Imago Dei*, which is Latin for the "Image of God."

Being made in the image of God does not mean you look like God physically. God is spirit, so He does not have a body like we do. Instead, it means you reflect His character. Just as a mirror reflects your face, you were built to reflect God to the world. You have the ability to create because God is the Creator. You have a sense of right and wrong because God is holy. You can speak and communicate because God is a talking God. You have the capacity for deep relationships because God exists in a perfect relationship as the Trinity.

This image of God gives every single person an incredible amount of worth. It does not matter if a person is old or young. It does not matter if they are rich or poor. It does not matter if they are healthy or sick. Every human being has "dignity." This means they deserve respect simply because they exist. When you see a person on the street who is struggling, you are looking at someone made in God's image. When you look at the person you find most annoying at school, you are looking at someone God carefully crafted. This truth should change how you treat everyone you meet.

God did not just make your spirit; He also made your body. Sometimes Christians act like the body is bad and only the soul is good. But that is not what the Bible teaches. God formed the first man out of the dust of the ground and breathed life into him. He made your eyes to see beauty and your ears to hear music. He made your hands to work and your feet to run. Your body is a gift. It is the temple of the Holy Spirit if you follow Jesus. This means how you treat your body matters. What you eat, how you sleep, and how you use your physical strength are all ways to honor God.

Why are we here? What is our job on this planet? God gave the first humans a "dominion mandate." This is a big phrase that just means we are God's representatives on earth. He put us here to take care of the world. We are meant to build things, grow things, and bring order to the chaos. You are not here just to wait for heaven. You are here to reflect God's light into every corner of the earth. Whether you become a doctor, a plumber, or a teacher, your job is to serve God and love people.

However, we have to be honest about one thing. The image of God in us is currently broken. Think of a mirror that has been dropped on the floor. It is still a mirror. It still reflects light. But the reflection is cracked and distorted. That is what happened when sin entered the world. We still have worth, but we also have a "sin nature." We use our words to hurt instead of heal. We use our creativity to make bad things. We forget our purpose and live for ourselves.

The good news is that God is in the business of fixing the mirror. Through Jesus, God is restoring His image in us. As you grow in your faith, you start to look more like the person you were always meant to be. You start to value people the way God does. You start to see yourself not as a failure or an accident, but as a beloved child of the King.

Do you ever feel like you don't fit in? Do you worry that you aren't "enough"? Remember that your value is not a score you have to earn. It is a gift you have already received. You were made on purpose, for a purpose. When you grasp this, you can stop trying to impress people. You can start living for the One who made you.

Apply and Act: Build a Healthy View of Yourself Based on God's Word

This section is designed to help you reject the lies of the world and embrace the truth about who God made you to be.

1. The "Image-Bearer" Audit

How do you see the people around you? Think about three people you interact with regularly. Write their names and one way you can see the "Image of God" in them (their creativity, their kindness, their sense of justice, etc.).

Person's Name	Evidence of God's Image
1.	
2.	
3.	

2. Body and Soul Balance

We are both physical and spiritual beings. Look at your habits from the last week.

- What is one thing you did to care for your **soul** (Example: Prayed, read the Bible)?

- What is one thing you did to care for your **body** (Example: Went for a run, got 8 hours of sleep)?

- Why do you think God cares about both of these things?

  ----

3. The Comparison Trap

We often feel bad about ourselves because we compare our "behind-the-scenes" life to everyone else's "highlight reel" on social media.

- List three things you often compare about yourself to others (Example: looks, grades, popularity).

  1. --
  2. --
  3. --

- Now, read **Psalm 139:13-16**. According to these verses, who is responsible for how you were "knit together"?

- How does this verse answer the three comparisons you listed above?

    ----

4. Word Study: Stewardship

Being a human means being a "steward" or a manager of God's world.

- List three "talents" or "skills" you have (Example: drawing, being a good listener, math).

    1. ____

    2. ____

    3. ____

- How can you use one of these skills to help someone else this week?

    ----

5. Real-Life Application: The "Respect Challenge"

Think of someone at school or in your community who is often ignored or treated poorly.

- Their Initials: _________

- **The Plan:** What is one small, respectful action you can take toward them this week to acknowledge their dignity as an image-bearer? (Example: Saying hello by name, sitting with them at lunch).

6. Guided Reflection Questions

Answer these in one or two clear sentences.

- If you truly believed that every person you met was made in the image of God, how would your social media comments change?

- Why is it important to know that you are a "broken" image-bearer and not a "perfect" one?

- What is the difference between "self-esteem" (feeling good about yourself) and "God-given worth"?

  ----

7. True or False?

Circle the correct answer based on what you have learned.

- **T / F:** Your value increases when you get better grades.
- **T / F:** Humans are the only part of creation made in God's image.
- **T / F:** The body is a "container" for the soul and does not really matter to God.
- **T / F:** Sin has completely destroyed the image of God in humans.
- **T / F:** Part of being human is having a job to do for God.

8. The "Why Am I Here?" Map

Think about your current life as a teen. Where has God placed you?

- **My Family:** One way I can reflect God here:

  ____

- **My School:** One way I can reflect God here:

  ____

- **My Friends:** One way I can reflect God here:

  ____

9. Identifying the Lies

What is the most common lie you tell yourself about your worth? (Example: "I am only valuable if I am successful.")

____

____

Find a Bible verse that contradicts that lie. (Hint: Use an index or search tool for words like "love," "worth," or "created").

Verse:

____

____

____

____

10. Memory Verse Challenge

Memorize **Genesis 1:27**: *"So God created man in his own image, in the image of God he created him; male and female he created them."* Write it out here from memory:

____

____

____

11. Final Action Step

Before you go to bed tonight, look in the mirror and say out loud: "I am made in the image of God, and I have a purpose."

- How does saying that make you feel?

----

12. A Prayer for Identity

"Father, thank You for making me. Thank You that I am not an accident. Help me to see the worth You have given me. Help me to see the worth in every person I meet today. Show me how to use my body and my mind to bring You glory. Amen."

CHAPTER 5

TURN FROM SIN (HAMARTIOLOGY)

Read and Learn: How Sin Breaks Things and Why We Need a Cure

The word "sin" is not very popular today. People prefer to use words like "mistake," "error," or "bad choice." These words make it sound like we just slipped up or tripped. But the Bible uses much stronger language. To understand why the world is a mess and why our own hearts feel restless, we have to look at the root of the problem. In theology, we call the study of sin "Hamartiology." This comes from the Greek word *hamartia*, which means "to miss the mark."

Imagine an archer aiming at a target. The goal is to hit the bullseye. If the arrow flies off to the side or falls short, the archer has missed the mark. God's "mark" for us is perfection. He created us to reflect His character and live in perfect harmony with Him. When we sin, we don't just "mess up." We fail to hit the target of God's holy standard. We fall short of His glory.

Where did this start? It began in a garden. In Genesis 3, we see the first humans, Adam and Eve, make a choice. God gave them everything they needed. He gave them one simple rule: do not eat from the tree of the knowledge of good and evil. But they chose to listen to a lie instead of the truth. They wanted to be like God. They wanted to set their own rules. This was the first act of rebellion. Since Adam was the head of the human race, his choice affected all of us. We are born with a "sin nature." This means we are not just sinners because we sin; we sin because we are sinners. It is part of our DNA from birth.

Sin shows up in two ways. First, there are "sins of commission." these are the bad things we do. It is the lie we tell to stay out of trouble. It is the mean comment we post online. It is the pride we feel when we think we are better than someone else. Second, there are "sins of omission." These are the good things we fail to do. It is when we see someone being bullied and say nothing. It is when we have the chance to help a neighbor but choose to play video games instead. Both types of sin are a rebellion against God.

Theology teaches us about "total depravity." This sounds like a scary phrase, but it is a simple idea. It does not mean that every person is as bad as they could possibly be. It means that every part of a person is touched by sin. Our minds think selfish thoughts. Our hearts love the wrong things. Our bodies are used for selfish goals. Even our "good" deeds are often done for the wrong reasons, like wanting praise from others. Sin is like a drop of ink in a glass of water. It spreads through the whole thing.

Why is sin such a big deal? It is a big deal because of who God is. Because God is perfectly holy, He cannot live in the presence of sin. Sin creates a huge gap between us and our Creator. It is like a wall that we cannot climb. The Bible says the "wages of sin is death." A wage is something you earn for your work. Because of our rebellion, we have earned a spiritual death. This means separation from God now and forever.

Sin also breaks our relationships with other people. When we are selfish, we hurt our friends. When we are dishonest, we break trust with our parents. Every war, every theft, and every broken heart in history can be traced back to sin. It is the great destroyer of peace. It makes us look at others as tools to get what we want instead of people made in God's image.

However, we cannot fix this on our own. You cannot "work off" your sin. You cannot be "good enough" to make up for the bad. If you are drowning in the middle of the ocean, you don't need a swimming lesson; you need a rescue. The law of God is like a mirror. It shows you that your face is dirty, but it cannot wash you. It shows you that you have missed the mark.

Recognizing our sin is the first step toward joy. If you don't know you are sick, you will never go to a doctor. If you don't know you are lost, you will never look at a map. When we admit that we have a sin problem, we are ready for the cure. God does not talk about sin to make us feel worthless. He talks about sin so we can see how much we need Jesus. The bad news of our sin makes the good news of the Savior even better.

This week, don't hide your struggles. Don't pretend you are perfect. Bring your mistakes into the light. When we face the truth about our sin, we find the path to real freedom.

Apply and Act: Track Your Habits and Ask for God's Help to Change

Use this section to look at your own life with honesty. Remember, God already knows your heart. He is ready to forgive and help you grow.

1. Missing the Mark

Think about the last 24 hours.

- List one "sin of commission" (something bad you did):

  ____

  ____

- List one "sin of omission" (something good you failed to do):

  ____

  ____

2. The Ripple Effect

Pick one of the sins you listed above. How did it affect other people?

- **Person affected:**

- **The result of the action:**

----

3. Scripture Search: The Definition of Sin

Read **1 John 3:4**.

- How does this verse define sin?

- Read **James 4:17**. How does this verse define sin?

----

4. The "Total Depravity" Check

How does sin affect these different parts of your life? Give a brief example for each.

- **Your Thoughts:**

- **Your Words:**

- **Your Use of Time:**

----

5. Identifying Patterns

Most of us have a "favorite" sin, a struggle that keeps coming back.

- What is one temptation you face almost every day? (Example: Anger, lying, laziness, lust).

- What is usually happening when you face this temptation? (Example: I am tired, I am with certain friends, I am bored on my phone).

____

____

6. The "Mirror" Exercise

Read the **Ten Commandments** in **Exodus 20:1-17**.

- Which commandment is the hardest for you to keep right now?

____

____

- Why do you think that specific rule is difficult for you?

____

____

7. Case Study: The "Small" Lie

Imagine you forgot to do your homework. Your teacher asks why it isn't finished. You think about saying your internet was down, even though it wasn't.

- Is this a "small" sin to God? Why or why not?

____

____

- What is the "mark" that you would be missing in this situation?

____

____

8. Guided Reflection Questions

Answer these in one or two sentences.

- Why do people often try to rename "sin" as a "mistake"?

____

____

- If God is holy, why can't He just ignore our sin?

____

____

- How does knowing you have a sin nature help you be more patient with other people's mistakes?

  ----

9. True or False?

- You are only a sinner if you do something really bad like murder. (________)
- Sin began with Adam and Eve in the garden. (________)
- We can fix our sin problem by doing enough good deeds. (________)
- Sin affects our minds, hearts, and bodies. (________)
- Every sin is a rebellion against God's authority. (________)

10. Real-Life Application: The Turning Point

The word for "turning from sin" is **repentance**. It means to change your mind and your direction.

- Pick one habit you want to change this week.

  The Habit:

- **The Turn:** Instead of doing that habit, what is one "holy" thing you can do instead? (Example: Instead of complaining, I will say one thing I am thankful for).

  ----

11. Memory Verse Challenge

Memorize **Romans 3:23**: *"For all have sinned and fall short of the glory of God."* Write it out three times below to help it sink in.

1. ____

2. ____

3. ____

12. The Prayer of Confession

Read **Psalm 51:1-4**. This was King David's prayer after he sinned greatly. Use it as a model to write your own short prayer of confession below.

----

13. Final Thought

If sin is a wall between us and God, who is the only one who can tear that wall down?

CHAPTER 6

LOVE THE SAVIOR (CHRISTOLOGY)

Read and Learn: Why Jesus Became a Man to Save His People

If you look at a timeline of human history, everything points to one Person. We even split time into two parts based on His birth. That Person is Jesus Christ. You might know His name from Sunday school or even from people using it as a curse word. But who is He really? In theology, we call this study "Christology." It is the most important topic you will ever study. If you get Jesus wrong, you get God wrong.

The first thing you must know is that Jesus is 100% God. He did not "become" God later in life. He did not just have "godly ideas." He is the eternal Son of God. He was there when the world was created. In fact, the Bible says everything was made through Him. He has all the traits of God that we talked about in Chapter 2. He is all-powerful, all-knowing, and holy. When you look at Jesus, you are looking at God in the flesh.

But here is the miracle: Jesus is also 100% man. This is called the "Incarnation." It means the Creator of the universe took on human skin. He became a baby in a manger. He grew up in a small town. He got hungry. He got tired. He felt physical pain. He even felt the sting of a friend's betrayal. Why did He do this? He did it because a human problem needed a human solution. Since a man (Adam) brought sin into the world, a man had to pay the price for that sin. Jesus had to be human so He could die in our place.

Jesus lived a perfect life. This is a very big deal. You and I "miss the mark" every single day. We fail at the target of holiness. But Jesus never missed once. He was tempted in every way that you are. He felt the pressure to fit in. He felt the pull of anger. But He never sinned. He kept every law of God perfectly. Because He had no sin of His own, He could take the punishment for yours.

Then came the cross. This was not an accident. It was not a tragedy where the "good guy" lost. It was a rescue mission. On the cross, a "divine exchange" happened. Jesus took all your lies, your pride, and your rebellion. He carried them on His shoulders. God treated Jesus as if He had lived your sinful life so that God could treat you as if you had lived Jesus' perfect life. He died the death you deserved to give you the life you could never earn.

If the story ended at the grave, we would still be lost. But three days later, Jesus walked out of the tomb. The resurrection is the proof that God accepted His sacrifice. It proves that Jesus is who He said He is. He beat death. He beat sin. He beat the devil. Today, He is alive. He is sitting at the right hand of God the Father. He is not just a figure from a history book. He is a King who is ruling right now.

Knowing about Jesus is not the same as knowing Him. You can know every stat about a pro athlete and still never meet them. You can know the lyrics to every song by a band and not know the lead singer. Jesus does not want fans; He wants followers. He wants to be the center of your life. He wants to be the one you turn to when you are lonely. He wants to be the one you thank when you are happy.

When you see how much Jesus loved you, it changes how you love others. It takes away your fear of the future. You don't have to prove your worth to anyone because the King of Kings already gave His life for you. You are loved with a love that will never let you go. This week, we will look at His life and see how His steps can guide your own.

Apply and Act: Follow the Steps of Jesus and Learn from His Life

This part of the chapter helps you see Jesus as a real Person who lived a real life. He is not a myth; He is your Savior.

1. The Two Natures of Jesus

We learned that Jesus is both God and Man. Read the verses below and identify which nature (Human or Divine) is being shown.

- **John 11:35** ("Jesus wept"):

- **Mark 4:39** (Jesus calms a storm with a word):

- **John 4:6** (Jesus was tired from his journey):

- **Matthew 9:6** (Jesus forgives sins):

  ----

2. The Life of Christ Timeline

Put these events from the life of Jesus in the correct order (1 to 6).

- [   ] The Resurrection
- [   ] The Baptism in the Jordan River
- [   ] The Birth in Bethlehem
- [   ] The Ascension to Heaven
- [   ] The Temptation in the Wilderness
- [   ] The Death on the Cross

3. Case Study: Temptation at School

Imagine a group of students is making fun of a teacher behind their back. They want you to join in. You feel the pressure to say something mean to fit in.

- Read **Hebrews 4:15**. How does knowing Jesus was tempted "in every way" help you in this moment?

- Since Jesus lived a perfect life, what kind of strength can He give you to say "no" to this group?

  ----

4. Word Study: Propitiation

This is a big word that means "a sacrifice that turns away anger."

- Read **1 John 2:2**. According to this verse, who is the sacrifice for our sins?

- How does it make you feel to know that Jesus took the "anger" or judgment that you earned?

  ----

5. The "I AM" Statements

In the book of John, Jesus uses the phrase "I AM" seven times to describe Himself. Look up these three and write what they mean to you.

- **John 8:12** ("I am the light of the world"):

- **John 10:11** ("I am the good shepherd"):

- **John 14:6** ("I am the way, the truth, and the life"):

  ----

6. Real-Life Application: Walking in His Steps

Pick one quality of Jesus that you saw in your reading this week (Example: He was kind to outcasts, He prayed often, He spoke the truth).

- **The Quality:**

- **The Plan:** How can you act like Jesus in this specific way at home or school tomorrow?

  ----

7. Guided Reflection Questions

Answer these briefly and directly.

- If Jesus were only a man and not God, why would His death not be enough to save everyone?

- If Jesus were only God and not a man, why would He not be able to understand your physical pain?

- Why is the resurrection (rising from the dead) the most important event in history?

  ----

8. The Exchange Check

Draw a line to match what Jesus took from us and what He gave back to us.

He Took: Our Sin   **He Gave:** His Peace

He Took: Our Shame   **He Gave:** His Righteousness (Perfection)

He Took: Our Death   **He Gave:** His Joy

He Took: Our Turmoil   **Gave:** His Eternal Life

9. Identifying Jesus in Your Day

Jesus said, "I am with you always."

- When did you feel like Jesus was "with you" today? (Example: During a hard test, while talking to a friend, while looking at nature).

____

____

10. Memory Verse Challenge

Memorize **John 1:14**: *"And the Word became flesh and dwelt among us, and we have seen his glory, glory as of the only Son from the Father, full of grace and truth."* Write it out here from memory:

____

____

____

11. A Letter to the Savior

Write a two-sentence "thank you" note to Jesus for what He did for you on the cross. Be specific about one thing He has changed in your life.

____

____

____

12. Final Action Step

Find one person this week who seems lonely or left out. Act as Jesus would by saying hello or including them.

Who will you look for?

____

13. Summary Question

Jesus asked His disciples, "Who do you say that I am?" If He asked you that question right now, what would your answer be?

____

____

____

____

CHAPTER 7

TRUST THE HELPER (PNEUMATOLOGY)

Read and Learn: How the Holy Spirit Gives You Strength and Peace

Imagine you are trying to build a massive skyscraper, but you only have a plastic hammer and a pair of scissors. No matter how hard you work, you simply do not have the power to finish the job. Many teens feel this way about their faith. They know what the Bible says, and they want to follow Jesus, but they feel like they lack the strength to actually do it. They try to be kind, but they get angry. They try to be pure, but their thoughts wander. They feel like they are running a race with no fuel in the tank.

The good news is that God did not leave you to live the Christian life on your own. When Jesus went back to heaven, He promised to send a "Helper." This Helper is the Holy Spirit. The study of the Holy Spirit is called "Pneumatology." This comes from the Greek word *pneuma,* which means "wind," "breath," or "spirit." Just as you cannot see the wind but you can see what it moves, you cannot see the Holy Spirit, but you can see the powerful ways He moves in a person's life.

The first thing to understand is that the Holy Spirit is a Person. He is not a "force" like gravity or electricity. He is not an "it." He is the third Person of the Trinity. He has a mind, He has feelings, and He has a will. The Bible says we can grieve Him when we sin and we can talk to Him in prayer. Most importantly, if you have put your trust in Jesus, the Holy Spirit lives inside you right now. You are His home.

What does the Holy Spirit actually do? First, He is the one who "convicts" us. This means He is the one who taps you on the shoulder when you are about to do something wrong. He gives you that "gut feeling" that a certain movie is bad for you or that a joke you made was mean. He doesn't do this to make you feel guilty and miserable; He does it to lead you back to the truth. He is like a coach who points out a mistake so you can play better next time.

Second, the Holy Spirit "illuminates" the Word of God. Have you ever read a Bible verse that made no sense, but then suddenly, it clicked? That was the Holy Spirit. He is the author of the Bible, so He is the best one to explain it. He helps you see how an ancient story about a shepherd boy actually applies to your stress at school today.

Third, the Holy Spirit produces "fruit." In Galatians 5, the Bible says that as we walk with the Spirit, our lives start to grow things like love, joy, peace, patience, kindness, and self-control. You cannot "manufacture" these things by trying harder. You cannot force yourself to be truly joyful when everything is going wrong. But the Spirit can grow those traits in you from the inside out. He changes what you want, not just what you do.

Finally, the Spirit gives "gifts." These are special abilities given to every believer to help the church. Some people are given the gift of teaching, others the gift of encouragement, and others the gift of serving or leadership. You have a spiritual gift that your church needs. The Spirit empowers you to do things for God that you could never do by yourself.

Living with the Holy Spirit means you never have to walk alone. You have a constant Friend, a powerful Counselor, and a steady Guide. When you feel weak, He is your strength. When you feel confused, He is your peace. To trust the Helper, you simply have to stop trying to do everything in your own power and start asking Him for His.

Apply and Act: Look for the Fruit of the Spirit in Your Own Actions

This section is designed to help you recognize the work of the Spirit in your daily life and learn how to listen to His lead.

1. The "Fruit" Inspection

Read **Galatians 5:22-23**. Look at the nine fruits listed there.

- Which of these fruits is currently the most visible in your life?

  ____

  ____

- Which of these fruits do you feel is "missing" or struggling to grow?

  ____

  ____

- Why do you think that specific fruit is hard for you right now?

  ____

  ____

2. Identifying Conviction

Think about a time in the last week when you felt a "tug" in your heart telling you that you were doing something wrong.

- **The Situation:**

  ____

- **The Feeling:**

  ____

- **The Result:** Did you listen to that tug or ignore it? What happened next?

  ____

  ____

  ____

3. Word Study: The Paraclete

Jesus called the Holy Spirit the *Paraclete*. This is a Greek word that means "one who walks alongside."

- Imagine you are walking through a dark, dangerous forest. How would having a "Paraclete" (a guide walking right next to you) change your level of fear?

- How can you remind yourself that the Spirit is "walking alongside" you at school tomorrow?

  ----

4. Gifts vs. Talents

A "talent" is something you are born with (like being good at piano). A "spiritual gift" is something the Spirit gives you to help others know God.

- What is one natural talent you have?

- How could the Holy Spirit use that talent as a "gift" to serve your church?

  ----

5. The "Illumination" Test

Pick a verse from the Bible that you find confusing. Write it here:

Now, pray a short prayer asking the Holy Spirit to help you understand it. Read it again. What is one new thought or "lightbulb moment" you had about that verse?

----

6. Real-Life Application: Walking by the Spirit

Walking by the Spirit means checking in with God before you react.

- **The Challenge:** Tomorrow, before you post anything on social media or send a text, pause for five seconds. Ask, "Holy Spirit, does this reflect Your fruit?"

- **The Goal:** To let the Spirit filter your words before they leave your fingers.

7. Case Study: The Exhausted Volunteer

Sarah is helping with the kids' ministry at her church. She is tired, she has a lot of homework, and she feels like quitting. She is trying to be "kind" to the kids, but she is losing her temper.

- Is Sarah relying on her own power or the Spirit's power?

- What is one specific prayer Sarah could pray to the Holy Spirit in that moment?

  ----

8. Guided Reflection Questions

Answer these briefly and directly.

- Why is it important to remember that the Holy Spirit is a Person and not just a "vibe" or a "feeling"?

- How does the Holy Spirit help you when you don't know what to pray for? (See **Romans 8:26**).

- What does it mean to "grieve" the Holy Spirit? (See **Ephesians 4:30**).

----

9. True or False?

- The Holy Spirit only comes to "super-Christians" or pastors. (________)
- You can have the Holy Spirit and still struggle with sin. (________)
- The Spirit's job is to make us look more like Jesus. (________)
- The Holy Spirit is less important than God the Father. (________)

10. Memory Verse Challenge

Memorize **Acts 1:8**: *"But you will receive power when the Holy Spirit has come upon you, and you will be my witnesses..."* Write the verse below and circle the word "power."

----

11. Identifying the Spirit's Voice

The Spirit usually speaks through the Bible or a quiet peace in our hearts. He never contradicts the Bible.

- If you have an idea to do something that the Bible says is wrong, is that the Holy Spirit speaking?

----

12. A Prayer for the Helper

"Holy Spirit, thank You for living in me. I admit that I have been trying to live in my own strength. Please grow Your fruit in my heart today. Help me to hear Your voice and give me the power to obey. Amen."

13. Final Thought

If the same Spirit who raised Jesus from the dead lives in you, is there any temptation in your life that is too strong for Him to beat?

CHAPTER 8

WALK IN SALVATION (SOTERIOLOGY)

Read and Learn: How Grace Changes Your Past, Present, and Future

In the world of sports, you have to earn your spot on the team. You have to practice hard, show up on time, and perform better than the next person. In school, you have to study to earn a good grade. Most of our lives are built on "if-then" systems: **if** you do the work, **then** you get the reward. Because of this, many people think God works the same way. They think they have to be "good enough" for God to like them. They hope that at the end of their lives, their good deeds will outweigh their bad ones.

But Christian theology teaches something completely different. This is the study of "Soteriology," which comes from the Greek word *soter*, meaning "savior" or "deliverer." It is the study of how God rescues us.

The most important thing to know about salvation is that it is a gift, not a paycheck. You do not earn it; you accept it.

Salvation happens in three "stages." Think of it as your past, your present, and your future.

First, there is **Justification**. This happens the very moment you put your faith in Jesus. In a courtroom, a judge might declare someone "not guilty." But God goes even further. He declares you "righteous." He takes your sin and gives you the perfection of Jesus. It is as if you have never sinned and have always obeyed. This solves your "past" problem. Your debt is paid, and you are officially a child of God. You are saved from the **penalty** of sin.

Second, there is **Sanctification**. This is what is happening right now. Once you are saved, God doesn't just leave you where you are. He begins a process of changing you from the inside out. He helps you hate the things He hates and love the things He loves. This is a slow process. You will still mess up, and you will still struggle. But over time, you should look more like Jesus than you did a year ago. You are being saved from the **power** of sin.

Third, there is **Glorification**. This is your future. When Jesus returns or when you go to be with Him after death, your struggle with sin will be over. You will receive a new body that never gets sick, and a heart that never wants to sin. You will be saved from the **presence** of sin.

How do you receive this gift? The Bible is very clear: it is by grace through faith. Grace means getting something good that you do not deserve. Faith is not just "believing that God exists." Even the demons believe that. Faith is **trust**. It is like sitting in a chair. You don't just believe the chair exists; you put your full weight on it. To have faith in Jesus means you stop trusting in your own "goodness" and put your full weight on what He did on the cross.

Many teens worry they can "lose" their salvation if they have a bad week. But if you didn't earn your salvation by being good, you can't lose it by being bad. Salvation is held together by God's power, not your effort. Because He started the work in you, He is the one who will finish it. This gives you the freedom to serve God out of love, not out of fear. You don't obey to **get** saved; you obey because you **are** saved.

This section is about moving salvation from a "head idea" to a "heart reality."

1. The Three Tenses of Salvation

Based on what you read, fill in the blanks below to see how God is working in your life.

- **Past:** I have been saved from the _________ of sin. (Justification)

- **Present:** I am being saved from the _________ of sin. (Sanctification)

- **Future:** I will be saved from the _________ of sin. (Glorification)

2. Grace vs. Merit

- **Merit:** Working a job for 10 hours and receiving $150.

- **Grace:** Having a debt of $1,000,000 and someone else paying it for you while giving you a gift on top of it.

- Which one describes your relationship with God?

    ____

    ____

- How does this make you feel about your "mistakes" from last week?

    ____

    ____

3. The "Chair" Test of Faith

Read **Ephesians 2:8-9**.

- According to these verses, can you brag about being a Christian? Why or why not?

    ____

    ____

- If salvation is a gift, what is the only thing you have to do to receive it?

    ____

    ____

4. Your Faith Story (Testimony)

A "testimony" is just a story of how you met Jesus. Even if it isn't "dramatic," it is powerful. Write one sentence for each part:

- **Before:** What was your life or attitude like before you trusted Jesus (or when you were younger)?

- **How:** How did you realize you needed a Savior?

- **After:** What is one way your life is different now that you know Him?

  ----

5. Practice the "Bridge" Illustration

Draw a simple picture here. On one side is a cliff labeled "People/Sin." On the other side is a cliff labeled "God/Holy." In the middle is a deep gap.

- How does Jesus act as the bridge between the two?

- Why can't we "jump" across the gap on our own?

  ----

6. Real-Life Application: The Assurance Check

Read **1 John 5:11-13**.

- Does God want you to "guess" if you are saved or "know" that you are saved?

- What is the "evidence" mentioned in verse 12?

  ----

7. Case Study: The "Good Guy" Friend

Your friend Alex is a great person. He is kind, gets straight A's, and volunteers. He says, "I don't need Jesus. I'm a good person, and God will see that."

- Based on **Romans 3:23** and what you learned about Justification, what is Alex missing?

- How could you kindly explain that even "good" people need a Savior?

  ----

8. Guided Reflection Questions

- If you knew for 100% certain that God would never leave you, how would that change the way you pray when you mess up?

- What is the difference between "feeling" saved and "being" saved?

  ----

9. True or False?

- Faith means I never have doubts.   (________)
- Justification is a one-time event.   (________)
- Sanctification is a process that takes a lifetime.   (________)
- I have to do more good things than bad things to
  go to heaven.   (________)

10. Memory Verse Challenge

Memorize **Romans 10:9**: *"Because, if you confess with your mouth that Jesus is Lord and believe in your heart that God raised him from the dead, you will be saved."* Write it out below:

  ----

11. A Prayer of Thanks

"Lord, thank You that my salvation does not depend on my performance. Thank You for the gift of Jesus. I trust Him as my Savior and my King. Help me to live this week out of gratitude for what You have already done. Amen."

12. Final Action Step

This week, tell one person (a parent, a friend, or a mentor) one thing you learned about God's grace.

- **Who will you tell?**

CHAPTER 9

SERVE THE CHURCH (ECCLESIOLOGY)

Read and Learn: Why the Church is a Team That Needs Your Help

When you hear the word "church," what is the first thing you picture? For some, it is a building with a tall steeple and stained-glass windows. For others, it is a boring hour on a Sunday morning where you have to wear uncomfortable clothes and sit still. Many people today think the church is an optional social club, something you attend if you have extra time or if your parents make you go. They see it as a place to "get" something: a good message, some music, or a chance to see friends.

But in the Bible, the church is never described as a building or a weekly event. The study of the church is called "Ecclesiology," from the Greek word *ekklesia*, which means "a called-out assembly." The church is a group of people who have been called out of the world to belong to Jesus. It is not a place you go; it is a family you belong to. It is not a performance you watch; it is a team you play on.

The Bible uses several powerful pictures to describe what the church is. One of the most famous is the **Body of Christ**. In 1 Corinthians 12, the apostle Paul explains that just as a human body has many parts, eyes, ears, hands, and feet, the church has many members. Each part has a different job, but every part is necessary. If the whole body were an eye, how would it hear? If the whole body were an ear, how would it smell? This means that you are a vital "organ" in the body of Jesus. If you are not there, or if you are not "functioning," the whole body suffers. You aren't just a spectator; you are a limb.

Another picture is the **Family of God**. When you trust in Jesus, God becomes your Father, which makes every other believer your brother or sister. This is why we often call people in church "Brother" or "Sister." This family is bigger than your DNA. It includes people of every age, every race, and every background. In a world where people are increasingly lonely, the church is meant to be a place where you are known, loved, and protected. You have "spiritual parents" to give you wisdom and "spiritual siblings" to walk through life with you.

The church is also called the **Temple of the Holy Spirit**. In the Old Testament, God's presence lived in a physical building made of stone and gold. Today, God lives in His people. When we gather together, God is present in a special way. We are like "living stones" being built into a house where God dwells. This makes the church holy and important. It is the place where heaven meets earth.

So, why does the church exist? It has a few main "assignments."

1. **Worship:** We gather to tell God how great He is.
2. **Discipleship:** We help each other grow in the Word and become more like Jesus.
3. **Fellowship:** We care for each other's needs, pray for each other, and eat together.
4. **Mission:** We work together to tell the world the Good News about salvation.

You might wonder, "Do I really need the local church? Can't I just follow Jesus on my own?" The answer from the Bible is a clear "no."

You cannot be a "lone wolf" Christian. A coal that is pulled out of the fire quickly goes cold. To stay on fire for God, you need the heat of other believers around you. You need people to encourage you when you are down and people to correct you when you start to wander away from the truth.

The local church also has a specific structure. God provides **pastors** and **elders** to lead and protect the "flock." He provides **deacons** to serve and meet practical needs. These leaders are there to "equip" you. Their job isn't to do all the work of the ministry; their job is to train *you* to do the work. Whether you are 13 or 30, you have a role to play.

Serving the church is one of the best ways to grow your faith. When you stop focusing on yourself and start focusing on helping others, you start to see God work in amazing ways. You might help in the nursery, run the soundboard, help set up chairs, or welcome visitors at the door. No job is too small for a servant of the King. When you serve, you aren't just helping the church; you are serving Jesus Himself.

The church is not perfect because it is filled with people like you and me—people who still struggle with sin. You will likely be let down by someone in a church at some point. You might find a service boring or a leader frustrating. But we don't give up on the church because it's imperfect. We stay committed because Jesus is committed to it. He calls the church His "Bride." He loves her, He died for her, and He is coming back for her. If the church is that important to Jesus, it should be that important to us.

Apply and Act: Pick a Way to Help Your Church Family This Week

This section will help you move from being a "customer" at church to being a "contributor."

1. The Body Part Inventory

In 1 Corinthians 12, Paul says every part of the body is important.

- If you had to describe yourself as a part of the body right now, which would you be? (Example: The "feet" because I like to go and do things; the "ears" because I am a good listener).

____

____

- Why did you pick that part?

  ----

2. Identifying Your Local Family

- Write down the name of your local church:

- Who are two adults in your church (besides your parents) that you look up to?

- Have you ever told them you appreciate them? If not, plan to do so this Sunday.

  ----

3. Word Study: Koinonia

The Bible uses the Greek word *koinonia* to describe the "fellowship" of the church. It means "sharing things in common."

- List three things you share in common with other people in your youth group or church.

  ----

4. The "One Another" Challenge

The New Testament has over 50 "one another" commands (e.g., "Love one another," "Encourage one another," "Pray for one another").

- Read **Hebrews 10:24-25.**
- According to these verses, what is the main reason we should not stop meeting together?

- How can you "stir up" a friend to do good works this week?

  ----

5. Service Scavenger Hunt

Look at the different ministries in your church. Put a checkmark next to any area where a teen could potentially help.

- [   ] Greeting/Welcoming people
- [   ] Helping with younger children
- [   ] Setting up or cleaning up events
- [   ] Music or Tech/Audio-Visual
- [   ] Cleaning the building or yard
- [   ] Visiting older members or sending cards

6. Real-Life Application: The First-Time Visitor Perspective

Imagine you are walking into your church for the very first time. You don't know anyone and you don't know where to go.

- What is one thing a teen in the church could do to make you feel welcome?

- Will you commit to doing that the next time you see someone new?

  ----

7. Case Study: The "I'm Bored" Dilemma

Your friend Tyler says, "I hate going to church. The music is old, the sermon is too long, and I don't get anything out of it. I'd rather just watch a YouTube preacher at home."

- Based on the "Body of Christ" idea, what is Tyler missing by staying home?

- How would you explain to Tyler that church isn't about "getting" something, but about "giving" something?

  ----

8. Guided Reflection Questions

- Why is it dangerous to think you can be a Christian without being part of a local church?

- How does the church act as a "hospital" for people who are hurting?

- What is one way your church could reach out to your school or neighborhood?

  ----

9. True or False?

- The church is a building where God lives.   (________)
- You are an important part of the body of Christ
  right now.   (________)
- Only pastors and elders are responsible for
  doing ministry.   (________)
- The church is a global family of all believers
  throughout history.   (________)

10. Memory Verse Challenge

- Memorize **1 Corinthians 12:27**: *"Now you are the body of Christ and individually members of it."* Write it out three times below:

  ----

11. The "Ask Your Pastor" Task

This week, find a leader at your church and ask them this question: "Is there a small way I can help out or serve this month?"

- **Who will you ask?**

- **What was their answer?**

----

12. A Prayer for Your Church

"Father, thank You for my church family. Thank You that I don't have to follow Jesus alone. Please protect our leaders and help us to love one another well. Show me where I can help and how I can use my gifts to serve You. Amen."

13. Final Thought

If the church is the "Bride of Christ," how should that change the way you talk about the church to your friends?

CHAPTER 10

CHANGE YOUR LIFE (SANCTIFICATION)

Read and Learn: How to Grow in Holiness by Following God's Rules

If you have ever started a workout routine or tried to learn a new language, you know that the first day is very different from the hundredth day. On day one, you make a decision. You sign the contract, you buy the shoes, or you download the app. But on day one hundred, you are a different person. Your muscles are stronger, or your vocabulary is larger. The initial decision was a one-time event, but the growth is a long-term process.

In your walk with God, something similar happens. In Chapter 8, we talked about *Justification*, that one-time event where God declares you "not guilty" because of Jesus. But once you are on the team, God begins the work of training you. This process is called **Sanctification**. It comes from the word "sanctify," which means to set something apart or to make it holy. Sanctification is the lifelong journey of becoming in your daily life what God has already declared you to be in His courtroom.

Sanctification is unique because it is a "cooperative" work. When it came to your salvation, Jesus did 100% of the work. You didn't help Him die on the cross, and you didn't help yourself be born again. However, in sanctification, God works and *you* work. The apostle Paul describes it this way: "Work out your own salvation with fear and trembling, for it is God who works in you" (Philippians 2:12-13). God provides the "want-to" and the power, but you have to provide the "do." You have to make the choices. You have to say "no" to the old habits and "yes" to the new ones.

So, how does this change actually happen? It isn't magic, and it usually doesn't happen overnight. God uses "means of grace", tools He has given us to help us grow.

1. The Word of God You cannot grow in holiness if you don't know what holiness looks like. The Bible acts as a light that shows you where the obstacles are. Jesus prayed, "Sanctify them in the truth; your word is truth" (John 17:17). As you read the Bible, it starts to scrub your mind. You stop seeing things through the world's eyes and start seeing them through God's eyes.

2. The Holy Spirit As we learned in Chapter 7, the Spirit is the "Helper." He is the engine of sanctification. He gives you a "holy nudge" when you are about to lose your temper. He gives you a sense of peace when you choose to tell the truth even when it's hard. Without the Spirit, sanctification is just "moralism", trying to be a good person to impress people. With the Spirit, it is a transformation of the heart.

3. Discipline and Habits Sanctification requires effort. This is where "God's rules" come in. We don't follow God's rules to *become* His children; we follow them because we *are* His children. Think of God's commands like the guardrails on a mountain road. They aren't there to stop you from having fun; they are there to keep you from driving off a cliff. When you practice disciplines like prayer, fasting, and church attendance, you are creating a space where God can change you.

4. Trials and Hard Times This is the part we usually don't like. Sometimes God uses difficult situations to "burn away" the things in us that shouldn't be there. Just as gold is heated in a fire to remove the dirt (impurities), our faith is often tested to make us stronger and more patient. When you face a hard time at school or a disappointment at home, God can use that to help you trust Him more than you trust yourself.

It is important to remember that sanctification is not about being "perfect." You will still have bad days. You will still struggle with the same sins you thought you defeated months ago. The goal of sanctification is not "perfection" in this life, but "direction." Is the general direction of your life moving toward Jesus? Are you more bothered by your sin today than you were last year? Do you love God more now than you used to?

A key part of this change is the "Put Off / Put On" principle found in Ephesians 4. Paul tells us to "put off" our old self, the lying, the anger, the selfishness, and to "put on" the new self, the truth-telling, the kindness, the hard work. You can't just stop a bad habit; you have to replace it with a good one. If you stop gossiping but don't start using your words to encourage people, there will be a hole in your heart that the gossip will eventually fill back up.

Change is hard, but you aren't doing it alone. The God who started the work in you is committed to finishing it. Every time you choose to be kind when you want to be mean, or honest when you want to lie, you are winning a small battle in the long war of sanctification. Keep going. The change is worth it.

Apply and Act: Set New Daily Habits That Honor God

Sanctification is about what you do when no one is looking. Use these exercises to build a plan for growth.

1. The "Direction" Check

Think about your life one year ago compared to today.

- What is one way you have grown in your faith?

- What is one sin or habit that you struggle with *less* now than you did then?

- What is one area where you feel "stuck"?

  ----

2. Put Off and Put On

Identify a "weed" in your heart (a bad habit) and a "seed" you want to plant (a good habit).

Put Off (The Weed)	Put On (The Seed)
Example: Complaining about school	*Example: Thanking God for the chance to learn*

3. Designing a "Rule of Life"

A "Rule of Life" is just a schedule of habits that keep you close to God. Fill in a simple plan for your week:

- **Daily:** When will I read the Bible and pray?

- **Weekly:** How will I serve or worship with others?

- **Monthly:** Is there something I can give up (like a fast from social media) to focus on God?

____

____

____

4. Word Study: Holiness

The word "Holy" (*hagios* in Greek) means "different" or "set apart."

- What is one thing you do during your week that makes you look "different" from your friends who don't follow Jesus?

____

____

- Is being "different" in that way a good thing or a bad thing? Why?

____

____

5. The "Means of Grace" Inventory

Which of these tools are you using the most right now? Which one do you need to pick up?

- [   ] **The Word:** I read it consistently.
- [   ] **Prayer:** I talk to God throughout the day.
- [   ] **Fellowship:** I have friends who push me toward Jesus.
- [   ] **The Sacraments:** I participate in Baptism and the Lord's Supper.

6. Real-Life Application: The Five-Minute Morning

For the next seven days, commit to spending the first five minutes of your day without your phone.

- **Minute 1-2:** Thank God for three specific things.

____

____

- **Minute 3-4:** Read a short Psalm.

____

____

- **Minute 5:** Ask the Holy Spirit to lead your choices today.

- **Check back:** How did this change your mood by lunchtime?

---

7. Case Study: The "Frustrated Christian"

Mark has been a Christian for two years. He is frustrated because he still gets angry very easily. He feels like he isn't "changing" enough, so he feels like giving up on church.

- Based on the "Direction vs. Perfection" idea, what would you say to Mark?

- How does knowing that sanctification is a "lifelong journey" help Mark?

---

8. Guided Reflection Questions

- Why does God give us "rules" or commands if we are already saved by grace?

- What is the difference between "trying" to be holy and "training" to be holy?

- How do your friends influence your sanctification (your growth in holiness)?

---

9. Identifying the Resistance

What is the biggest "distraction" that keeps you from growing spiritually? (Example: Gaming, social media, sports, sleep).

How can you put a "guardrail" around that distraction this week?

----

10. Memory Verse Challenge

Memorize **1 Thessalonians 4:3**: *"For this is the will of God, your sanctification..."* Write it out three times and keep it in your pocket today.

----

11. The "Holy" Habit Tracker

Pick one small habit (like praying before you eat or reading one verse before bed). Mark a checkbox for every day you do it this week.

- M   [ ]
- T   [ ]
- W   [ ]
- T   [ ]
- F   [ ]
- S   [ ]
- S   [ ]

12. A Prayer for Growth

"Lord, I want to change. I don't want to stay the same person I am today. Thank You for loving me as I am, but thank You for not leaving me as I am. Please give me the strength to put off my old selfish ways and put on Your love and truth. Make me holy, as You are holy. Amen."

13. Final Thought

If sanctification is a team effort between you and God, who is responsible if you aren't growing? Who is responsible for the power to grow?

CHAPTER 11

FACE THE ENEMY (ANGELOLOGY/SPIRITUAL WARFARE)

Read and Learn: Understanding the Unseen World and Finding Victory

Most of the time, we focus only on what we can see: our friends, our homework, our phones, and our families. But the Bible tells us that there is an entire world existing right alongside ours that is completely invisible to the human eye. This is the spiritual realm. Just because you can't see it doesn't mean it isn't real. In fact, the things happening in the unseen world often drive the things happening in the visible world.

The study of this realm is called **Angelology** (the study of angels) and **Demonology** (the study of fallen angels). Understanding this isn't about being scared or becoming obsessed with ghost stories. It's about being prepared. If you were walking into a literal battlefield but didn't believe there was an enemy, you would be in serious trouble.

The Good Guys: Angels

Angels are created spiritual beings. They are not "humans who died and got wings." They were created before the world began to serve God and care for His people. They are incredibly powerful, intelligent, and fast. The Bible shows them doing several things:

- **Worshiping God:** They constantly surround God's throne, singing of His holiness.

- **Delivering Messages:** The word "angel" literally means "messenger." They brought the news of Jesus' birth and told the disciples He had risen.

- **Protecting Believers:** Psalm 91 says God commands His angels to guard you. They often step in to help us in ways we don't even realize until later.

The Bad Guys: Demons and Satan

Not all spiritual beings stayed on God's side. Long ago, a high-ranking angel named Lucifer (Satan) became proud. He wanted to be God rather than serve God. He led a rebellion, and a third of the angels fell with him. These are now known as demons.

Satan is not God's equal. He is a created being, which means he is on a leash. He is not all-knowing or all-powerful. However, he is a master of deception. The Bible calls him the "Father of Lies" and the "Accuser." His goal is simple: to steal, kill, and destroy. He wants to destroy your relationship with God, your reputation, and your joy.

The Battle: Spiritual Warfare

Because you belong to Jesus, you are a target. This isn't meant to frighten you, but to wake you up. You are in a spiritual war. However, this war isn't fought with tanks and guns. It is fought in your mind and your heart.

The "front lines" of spiritual warfare usually look like:

- **Lies:** The enemy whispers that you aren't good enough, that God is holding out on you, or that "just once" won't hurt.

- **Discouragement:** Making you feel like giving up on your faith or your church.

- **Division:** Stirring up drama between you and your parents or friends.

The Victory: The Armor of God

In Ephesians 6, the Bible tells us exactly how to fight back. We are told to "put on the full armor of God."

1. **The Belt of Truth:** Knowing what God says is true so you can spot the enemy's lies.

2. **The Breastplate of Righteousness:** Protecting your heart by living a life that honors God.

3. **The Shoes of Peace:** Being ready to share the Gospel and staying calm in the chaos.

4. **The Shield of Faith:** Trusting God's promises to "extinguish" the flaming arrows of doubt.

5. **The Helmet of Salvation:** Protecting your mind by remembering you belong to Jesus.

6. **The Sword of the Spirit:** The Word of God. This is your only offensive weapon. When Jesus was tempted by Satan, He didn't argue; He quoted Scripture.

The most important thing to remember is that the war is already won. Jesus defeated Satan at the cross. The enemy is like a defeated army that is still causing trouble as it retreats. You don't fight *for* victory; you fight *from* victory. Because the Holy Spirit is in you, you have more power than any demon in existence. "He who is in you is greater than he who is in the world" (1 John 4:4).

Apply and Act: Recognize the Lies and Put on Your Armor

This section helps you move from being a victim of the enemy's schemes to being a soldier in God's kingdom.

1. Identifying the "Arrows"

Satan often uses "flaming arrows" of thoughts to get us off track. Which of these "arrows" have you felt this week? (Check all that apply).

- [ ] "God is disappointed in you because of what you did."

- [ ] "You're the only one who actually cares about this stuff."

- [ ] "One little lie won't matter; everyone does it."

- [ ] "You'll never be as good a Christian as [Name]."

- [ ] "Is the Bible even really true?"

2. Using the Sword

Pick one of the arrows you checked above. Find a "Sword" (a Bible verse) that cuts through that lie.

- **The Lie:**

- **The Truth (Bible Verse):**

  ----

3. The Reality Check

Read **2 Kings 6:15-17**.

- What did Elisha's servant see at first?

- What did he see after Elisha prayed for his eyes to be opened?

- How does this story change how you feel when you feel "outnumbered" at school?

  ----

4. Word Study: The Accuser

The name "Satan" actually means "Accuser." He likes to remind you of your sins to make you feel too dirty to pray.

- Read **Romans 8:1**. If you are in Christ, is there any condemnation left for you?

- Next time you feel "accused" of a past sin, what will you tell the enemy?

  ----

5. Daily Armor Drill

Before you leave the house tomorrow, literally go through the motions of putting on the armor.

- **The Belt:** "God, help me speak and believe the truth today."
- **The Breastplate:** "Protect my heart from doing things I know are wrong."
- **The Shoes:** "Make me a peacemaker at school today."
- **The Shield:** "I trust You even if things get hard today."
- **The Helmet:** "Thank You that I am saved and I am Yours."
- **The Sword:** "Remind me of Your Word when I am tempted."

6. Case Study: The "Just a Little" Temptation

Your friends are planning to sneak out or do something you know your parents wouldn't allow. You feel a massive amount of pressure to go. You start thinking, "God will forgive me anyway, and I want to have fun."

- Is this just your thought, or could it be a spiritual attack?

- Which piece of armor do you need most in this moment?

- What is the "Sword of the Spirit" (verse) you can use to stay strong?

  ----

7. Guided Reflection Questions

- Why is it dangerous to be *too* afraid of the devil?

- Why is it dangerous to *ignore* the reality of the devil?

- What is the difference between an angel and a human?

____

____

8. True or False?

- Angels are the spirits of people who have died.   (________)
- Satan can read your mind.   (________)
- We have the power to defeat the enemy because of Jesus.   (________)
- Spiritual warfare is mostly about scary movies and exorcisms.   (________)

9. Identifying the "Strongholds"

A "stronghold" is a pattern of thinking that is hard to break. (Example: "I have to be perfect for people to like me.")

- Is there a "stronghold" in your mind that the enemy uses to keep you unhappy?

____

____

- How can the "Truth" (the Belt) set you free from that?

____

____

10. Memory Verse Challenge

Memorize **James 4:7**: *"Submit yourselves therefore to God. Resist the devil, and he will flee from you."* Note the order: you must submit to God *before* you can successfully resist the devil. Write it here:

____

____

11. A Prayer for Protection

"Lord, thank You that the victory is already Yours. I put on Your armor today. Protect my mind from lies and my heart from evil. Send Your angels to guard me and my family. Help me to stand firm in my faith and to use Your Word to fight back against temptation. Amen."

12. Final Thought

If you are on the winning team, why do we sometimes act like we are losing? How can you live like a "victor" this week?

CHAPTER 12

WAIT FOR THE KING (ESCHATOLOGY)

Read and Learn: Why the End of the Story is the Best Part

If you have ever read a long book or watched a movie series, you know that the ending is what gives the whole story meaning. If a hero dies for no reason, or if the villain wins and everyone stays sad, the story feels broken. But if the hero returns, the broken things are fixed, and the characters find a home, the ending makes the earlier struggles worth it.

The study of the "end times" or the "last things" is called **Eschatology**. It comes from the Greek word *eschatos*, which means "last." For many people, this topic feels scary. They think about world-ending disasters, mysterious beasts, and a "Great Tribulation." But for a follower of Jesus, eschatology isn't a horror movie. It is a love story. It is the promise that the King who left is coming back to claim His people and set the world right.

The Return of the King

The most important event in the future is the **Second Coming of Christ**. When Jesus left the earth after His resurrection, the angels told the disciples, "This Jesus, who was taken up from you into heaven, will come in the same way as you saw him go into heaven" (Acts 1:11).

Unlike His first coming, where He arrived as a quiet baby in a humble manger, His second coming will be loud, visible, and unmistakable. Every eye will see Him. He is not coming back to be judged; He is coming back to judge. He is not coming back to die; He is coming back to rule. For those who love Him, this is the most exciting day in history. It means that the war with sin and the devil is finally over.

The Resurrection of the Body

One of the most amazing parts of eschatology is what happens to *us*. The Bible teaches that when Jesus returns, there will be a "resurrection of the dead." This doesn't mean we will be floating clouds or ghosts in white robes. It means our physical bodies will be brought back to life, but they will be better.

In 1 Corinthians 15, Paul calls our current bodies "seeds." A seed is small and brown, but when it grows, it becomes a beautiful flower or a strong tree. Our "resurrection bodies" will be like Jesus' body after He rose. We will be able to eat, walk, and talk, but we will never get sick, we will never grow old, and we will never die again. The "brokenness" you feel in your body or your mind today is temporary.

The Final Judgment

The Bible is also honest about the fact that there is a day of accounting. God is a perfectly just Judge. He cannot let evil go unpunished forever. There will be a Final Judgment where every secret is brought into the light.

- **For those who rejected Jesus:** This is a day of great sadness. Without the "bridge" of Jesus (which we talked about in Chapter 8), they must pay the penalty for their own sins, which is eternal separation from God in a place the Bible calls Hell.

- **For those who trust Jesus:** This is not a day of fear. Because Jesus already took their punishment on the cross, they are welcomed into the Kingdom. Their "works" will be tested, not to see if they get into heaven, but to receive rewards for how they served God.

A New Heaven and a New Earth

Many people think that "Heaven" is just a place in the clouds where we sit on harps. But the Bible's ending is much better than that. In Revelation 21, John sees a "New Heaven and a New Earth." God is going to "make all things new."

Imagine the most beautiful place you have ever been—a mountain lake, a lush forest, or a perfect sunset. Now, imagine that place without any trash, any pollution, any sadness, or any mosquitoes! The New Earth will be a physical world where we live with God. There will be no more cancer, no more school shootings, no more depression, and no more funerals. "He will wipe away every tear from their eyes, and death shall be no more" (Revelation 21:4).

How Do We Wait?

Since we know the ending, how should we live today? We shouldn't be obsessed with trying to guess the exact date Jesus will return (Jesus said even He didn't know the day or hour!). Instead, we should live with **Urgency** and **Hope**.

- **Urgency:** We want to tell our friends about Jesus now, because we know the story has an end.

- **Hope:** When we go through hard times, bullying, family problems, or health issues, we remember that the "best part" hasn't started yet. We are like people standing in the rain who know that a warm house and a feast are waiting for them just around the corner.

The very last prayer in the Bible is simple: *"Amen. Come, Lord Jesus!"* (Revelation 22:20). That should be our prayer too.

Eschatology is meant to change your "now," not just your "later." Use these activities to focus your heart on the coming King.

1. The "Wipe Away" List

Read **Revelation 21:1-5**.

- List three things that exist in our world today that will *not* exist in the New Earth.

    1. ____

    2. ____

    3. ____

- Which one are you most excited to see gone? Why?

    ____

    ____

2. Word Study: Maranatha

In the early church, Christians used the word "Maranatha" as a greeting. It is an Aramaic word that means "Our Lord, come!"

- Why do you think people today are sometimes *afraid* for Jesus to come back?

- How can you shift your mindset from "I'm scared of the end" to "Maranatha"?

3. The "Resurrection Body" Reflection

If you could ask God for one thing to be "healed" or "fixed" in your resurrection body (a disability, a scar, a mental struggle), what would it be?

    ____

    ____

Take a moment to thank God that a day is coming when that struggle will be gone forever.

4. Identifying the Signs

Jesus gave us some "birth pains" to look for that show the end is approaching (Matthew 24).

- [ ] Wars and rumors of wars
- [ ] Famines and earthquakes
- [ ] People's love growing cold
- [ ] The Gospel being preached to all nations
- Do you see any of these happening in the news today?

---

5. Real-Life Application: Living with Urgency

If you knew for a fact that Jesus was returning this Friday, what is one thing you would do differently this week?

- Why wait until the end? Can you do that one thing *this* week?

---

6. Case Study: The "Depressed" Christian

Your friend Chloe is going through a really hard time. Her parents are getting a divorce, and she says, "Everything is falling apart. There's no point in trying because the world is just going to get worse anyway."

- How does the "New Heaven and New Earth" promise give Chloe a reason to keep going?

- How would you explain that our suffering today is "light and momentary" compared to the glory that is coming? (See **2 Corinthians 4:17**).

---

7. The Reward System

Read **1 Corinthians 3:12-15**.

- The Bible says our work for God is like "gold, silver, and precious stones." What is one "work" you did this week that you think God would consider "precious"? (Example: Helping a sibling, praying for a teacher).

8. Guided Reflection Questions

- What is the difference between "Heaven" and the "New Earth"?

- Why is it important that Jesus comes back *physically* and not just "in our hearts"?

- How does knowing the end of the story help you when you see bad news on the internet?

  ----

9. True or False?

- We will become angels when we die.   (_______)
- No one knows the exact date when Jesus will return.   (_______)
- The New Earth will be a place where we can do physical activities like eating and working.   (_______)
- Hell is a place of eternal separation from God.   (_______)

10. Memory Verse Challenge

Memorize **Revelation 21:4**: *"He will wipe away every tear from their eyes, and death shall be no more, neither shall there be mourning, nor crying, nor pain anymore, for the former things have passed away."* Write it out here:

----

11. The "Kingdom" Habit

Jesus told us to pray, "Your Kingdom come, Your will be done, on earth as it is in heaven."

- What is one way you can bring a "little bit of heaven" to your school or home today? (Example: Being a peacemaker in an argument).

----

12. A Prayer for the Return

"Lord Jesus, thank You that the story doesn't end with sin and death. Thank You that You are coming back to fix every broken thing. Help me to live with hope today. Give me the courage to tell others about Your Kingdom. We join the voices of the saints and say: Maranatha! Come, Lord Jesus! Amen."

13. Final Thought

At the end of the Bible, God says, "Behold, I am making all things new." What is the one thing in your life you most want Him to make new?

CONCLUSION
KEEP GOING

Read and Learn: The End of the Book is the Beginning of the Journey

Congratulations. You have arrived at the final pages of this journey. If you have read through the previous twelve chapters, you have done something that many adults never do: you have built a systematic framework for your faith. You have traveled from the mountaintop of *Theology Proper* (who God is) to the valley of *Hamartiology* (the problem of sin), and you have looked forward to the glorious sunrise of *Eschatology* (the return of the King). You now possess a map of the Christian faith. You know where the roads lead, where the dangers lie, and where the treasure is buried.

However, there is a massive difference between owning a map and actually taking the trip. You can study a map of Paris for years—memorizing the street names, the location of the Eiffel Tower, and the best places to get a croissant—but until you actually step onto a plane and walk the streets, you haven't truly experienced Paris. In the same way, theology is the map, but the Christian life is the journey. You have spent this time studying the map so that you can walk the road with confidence. But the map is not the destination. God is the destination.

This conclusion is not really an ending; it is a commissioning. It is a "send-off." In graduation ceremonies, the final speech is often called the "Commencement Address." "Commencement" means "beginning." You are graduating from this basic study, but you are commencing a lifetime of walking with Jesus. As you close this book and step back into your normal life—with its homework, social drama, sports practices, and family dynamics—there are several critical truths you must carry with you to ensure that you don't just *start* well, but that you *keep going.*

The Danger of the "Big Head, Small Heart"

The first danger you face now that you know some theology is pride. The Bible warns us in 1 Corinthians 8:1 that "knowledge puffs up, but love builds up." There is a trap that many young theologians fall into. They learn big words like *Justification, Inerrancy,* and *Omniscience.* They learn the arguments against atheism and the errors of other religions. And suddenly, they feel superior. They start to use their theology like a club to beat people over the head rather than a light to guide them home.

You might find yourself sitting in a small group or a Sunday school class, listening to someone say something that isn't *quite* theologically correct. The temptation will be to jump in, correct them, and show off what you know. But remember this: The devil is a better theologian than you are. He knows the Bible better than you do. He knows exactly who Jesus is (James 2:19 says the demons believe and shudder). The difference is that the devil has a massive amount of knowledge and zero love. He has a big head and a shriveled heart.

True theology should always lead to *Doxology* (worship) and *Missiology* (mission). If your study of God makes you love people less, you have studied wrong. If learning about God's holiness makes you arrogant rather than humble, you have missed the point. As you move forward, check your heart. Is your knowledge fueling your love? Are you becoming kinder, more patient, and more gracious? The greatest theologians in history were not the ones who won the most debates; they were the ones who looked the most like Jesus.

The Spiral of Faith: Learning the Same Truths Deeper

One of the misconceptions about growing in faith is that you "master" a topic and move on. You might think, "I already did Chapter 2 on God's attributes. I know that God is love. What's next?" But the Christian life is not a straight line where you leave the basics behind. It is a spiral. You circle back to the same truths over and over again, but each time, you go deeper.

- **Level 1:** When you are 5 years old, you learn "Jesus loves me." It makes you feel safe in the dark.

- **Level 2:** When you are 15 (right now), you learn "Jesus loves me" means He died on the cross to pay for your sins (Atonement). It helps you deal with guilt and shame.

- **Level 3:** When you are 25 and perhaps face a career failure or a broken engagement, you will need to learn "Jesus loves me" in a new way—that His love is your identity, not your success.

- **Level 4:** When you are 50 and perhaps lose a parent or face a health crisis, "Jesus loves me" will become the rock that keeps you from despair.

- **Level 5:** When you are on your deathbed, "Jesus loves me" will be the only thing that matters as you prepare to meet Him.

It is the same truth, but the depth is infinite. Never feel like you are "too advanced" for the basics. The Gospel is not the ABCs of Christianity; it is the A to Z. You never graduate from the cross. You just see more of its beauty the longer you stare at it.

The Long Obedience in the Same Direction

We live in a world of instant gratification. We want 2-minute noodles, 30-second TikToks, and same-day delivery. We are used to things happening fast. But spiritual growth is slow. It is more like growing an oak tree than downloading an app. There will be seasons in your life where you feel "on fire" for God. You will come back from a summer camp or a retreat feeling like you could conquer the world. You will read your Bible for an hour a day and pray with passion.

But then, February comes. The "spiritual high" wears off. You get tired. God feels distant. The Bible feels boring. You might wonder, "Did I lose my faith? Is something wrong with me?"

This is normal. Faith is not a feeling; it is a commitment. Eugene Peterson called the Christian life "a long obedience in the same direction." It is easy to be a Christian when the music is playing and everyone is emotional. It is hard to be a Christian on a Tuesday morning when you failed a test and your friends are being mean. But that is where real faith is forged.

"Keep Going" means you develop **Holy Habits**. You don't brush your teeth only when you feel inspired by dental hygiene; you do it because you want to keep your teeth. In the same way, you don't read the Bible only when you feel "spiritual"; you read it because you need to eat. You don't go to church only when you like the preacher; you go because you need the family. When the feelings fade, the habits hold you.

Think of a train. The engine is **Fact** (the truth of God's Word). The coal car is **Faith** (your trust in the engine). The caboose is **Feeling**. If you try to let the caboose pull the train, you will go nowhere. Feelings follow facts and faith. Don't let your emotions drive the train. Keep shoveling the coal of faith into the engine of truth, even when you don't feel like it. The feelings will eventually catch up.

Facing the inevitable Doubts

As you get older, you will face questions you haven't thought of yet. You might go to college and have a professor who mocks the Bible. You might see a tragedy on the news and wonder, "How can a good God allow this?" You might have a prayer that goes unanswered for years.

When this happens, do not panic. Doubt is not the opposite of faith. Silence is the opposite of faith. Doubt can actually be a growing pain. It is your mind trying to fit a big God into a small box. When the box breaks, it feels scary, but it means you are ready for a bigger view of God.

When you doubt:

1. **Don't doubt alone.** The worst thing you can do is isolate yourself. Talk to a parent, a pastor, or a wise mentor. Tell them, "I'm struggling with X." You will likely find that they have struggled with it too.

2. **Doubt your doubts.** We often question God, but we rarely question our own questions. Why do you feel this way? Is it

because of a fact, or because of a disappointment? Are you doubting God because the evidence is bad, or because you want to live a certain way that God forbids?

3. **Keep eating.** If you are sick and lose your appetite, you still have to eat to get better. If you are spiritually sick with doubt, don't stop reading the Bible or praying. Keep feeding your soul while you look for answers.

The Mission: You Are a Theologian Now

Finally, remember that this theology is not for you to keep in a jar. It is for you to share. You are now a carrier of the cure. The world is sick with sin. People are confused about who they are, why they are here, and where they are going. You have the answers to the test. You know the Creator. You know the Savior. You know the end of the story.

You don't have to be a preacher to share this. You just have to be a witness. A witness in a courtroom doesn't have to argue the case or convince the jury; they just have to tell what they saw and heard. "I was lost, and Jesus found me. I was anxious, and He gave me peace. I was guilty, and He forgave me." That is your testimony.

As you go into high school, college, and your career, you are an ambassador of the Kingdom of Heaven. When you are honest when everyone else cheats, you are doing theology. When you are kind to the person everyone else ignores, you are doing theology. When you forgive someone who hurt you, you are showing them the Cross.

The Final Charge

In the book of Hebrews, the author gives us a picture of a great race. He says we are surrounded by a "great cloud of witnesses", all the believers who have gone before us. Moses, David, Esther, Peter, Paul, your grandmother who prayed for you—they are all in the stands of the stadium, cheering you on.

They are shouting, "Keep going! It's worth it! The struggle is temporary, but the glory is eternal! Don't give up!"

Jesus is at the finish line. He is the "founder and perfecter of our faith." He ran the race first to show us how. He endured the cross for the joy set before Him. Now, it is your turn to run.

Don't run to earn His love; run because you already have it.

Don't run to get saved; run because you are saved.

Don't run alone; run with the Church.

Take the map you have built in these 12 chapters. Put it in your backpack. Tie your shoes. Look at the finish line.

Ready? Set?

Keep Going.

This final application section is different. It is not just for this week. It is a set of tools and plans for the rest of your life. This is your survival kit for the long journey ahead.

1. The "Theology in Real Life" Future Forecast

Let's look at how the specific doctrines you learned will help you in future adult situations. Fill in the blanks with how you think that truth will apply.

Future Scenario	Relevant Doctrine	How this Truth Will sustain You
First College Class attacks the Bible	*Bibliology (Inerrancy)*	*I will know that the Bible is historically reliable and God's Word, so I won't be shaken by one professor's opinion.*
You feel lonely in a new city	*Theology Proper (Omnipresence)*	
You mess up big time at a job	*Soteriology (Justification)*	

A loved one gets very sick	*Eschatology (Resurrection)*	
You don't know who to marry/date	*Pneumatology (Guidance)*	

2. The "Spiritual Emergency" Kit

Write down 5 Bible verses that will be your "Emergency Contacts" when things get tough. Memorize these.

1. **For Anxiety:** (e.g., Philippians 4:6-7)

   ____

2. **For Guilt:** (e.g., 1 John 1:9)

   ____

3. **For Loneliness:** (e.g., Psalm 23)

   ____

4. **For Temptation:** (e.g., 1 Corinthians 10:13)

   ____

5. **For Doubt:** (e.g., Mark 9:24)

   ____

3. The "3-Year-Old" Challenge

Albert Einstein said, "If you can't explain it simply, you don't understand it well enough."

- Imagine a 3-year-old asks you: "Who is Jesus?"
- Write a 2-sentence answer using the theology you learned (Christology), but simple enough for a toddler.

   ____
   ____
   ____

4. Developing Your "Rule of Life" (Expanded)

We touched on this in Chapter 10, but let's make a sustainable plan for the "Long Obedience."

- **The Intake:** I will read the Bible for ____ minutes per day, at this time: __________.

- **The Outpour:** I will serve others/church ____ times per month.

- **The Rest:** I will take a "Sabbath" (rest from work/school) on this day: __________.

- **The Community:** I will meet with other Christians for encouragement (Youth Group/Small Group) on this day: __________.

5. Case Study: The Deconstruction

You have a friend named Taylor. After high school, Taylor stops going to church and posts on Instagram: "I'm deconstructing my faith. The church is full of hypocrites, and I don't think God is real anymore."

- **Empathy:** How do you respond with love instead of judgment?

  ____

  ____

- **Theology:** How does your knowledge of *Ecclesiology* (the church is made of broken sinners) help you explain why hypocrites exist without disproving God?

  ____

  ____

- **Action:** What is the best way to "witness" to Taylor in this season? (Hint: Is it an argument or a friendship?)

  ____

  ____

6. The "Doxology" Reflection

Read the lyrics to the "Doxology" below. This is a short hymn sung by the church for hundreds of years.

"Praise God from whom all blessings flow; Praise Him all creatures here below; Praise Him above ye heavenly host; Praise Father, Son, and Holy Ghost. Amen."

- **Father:** Why do you praise Him?

- **Son:** Why do you praise Him?

- **Holy Ghost:** Why do you praise Him?

  ----

7. The "Ebenezers" (Stones of Remembrance)

In the Old Testament, Samuel set up a stone and called it "Ebenezer," saying, "Thus far the Lord has helped us."

- Look back at your life so far. List three specific times God helped you, answered a prayer, or guided you.

  1. ____

  2. ____

  3. ____

- Whenever you doubt God in the future, come back and read this list.

  ----

8. Recommended Reading List (The Next Steps)

You finished this intro book. Here are three types of books to look for next to keep growing:

- **A Biography:** Read about a missionary or a saint (like *The Hiding Place* by Corrie ten Boom or *Through Gates of Splendor* by Elisabeth Elliot).

- **A Devotional:** Something to help you pray (like *My Utmost for His Highest* or *New Morning Mercies*).

- **A Deeper Theology Book:** (Ask your pastor for a recommendation suited to your age).

9. The Great Commission Contract

Read **Matthew 28:18-20**. This is your job description.

- **"Go"**: Where is your current "mission field"? (School, team, neighborhood).

- **"Make Disciples"**: Who is one person you can invite to church or read the Bible with?

- **"I am with you always"**: How does this promise give you the courage to sign your name below?

Signed (Your Name): ___________________________

Date: _______________________________________

A Final Letter to the Reader

Dear Friend,

If we were sitting across from each other at a coffee shop right now, I would tell you that I am proud of you. Studying God is the hardest and most rewarding work you can do.

But I would also tell you that the best days are ahead of you. Following Jesus is an adventure. It is not safe, He is, as C.S. Lewis wrote, "not a tame lion." He will ask you to do hard things. He will ask you to forgive people who don't deserve it. He will ask you to give your money and your time to help the poor. He will ask you to stand up for the truth when it costs you popularity.

But He will also give you a joy that the world cannot understand. He will give you a peace that makes no sense in the middle of a storm. He will give you a purpose that is bigger than making money or being famous. He will give you Himself.

Don't settle for a shallow faith. Don't settle for a "Sunday-only" religion. Dive into the deep end. Read the hard parts of the Bible. Pray big prayers. Love the unlovable.

You have the map. You have the gear. You have the Guide.

Keep Going.

To help you review, here is a quick "Cheat Sheet" of the big theological words we covered in this book. Keep this handy!

The Word	The Chapter	The Simple Definition
Bibliology	Ch 1	The study of the Bible; how God speaks to us.
Revelation	Ch 1	God showing us who He is (General: Nature; Special: Bible/Jesus).
Inerrancy	Ch 1	The Bible is completely true and without error in what it teaches.
Theology Proper	Ch 2	The study of God the Father and His attributes.
Trinity	Ch 3	God is One in essence, but Three in Person (Father, Son, Spirit).
Anthropology	Ch 4	The study of humanity; we are made in the Image of God (*Imago Dei*).
Hamartiology	Ch 5	The study of sin; "missing the mark."
Christology	Ch 6	The study of Jesus; fully God and fully man.

The Word	The Chapter	The Simple Definition
Incarnation	Ch 6	God becoming flesh (Jesus being born).
Atonement	Ch 6	Jesus paying the penalty for our sin on the cross.
Pneumatology	Ch 7	The study of the Holy Spirit; the Helper.
Soteriology	Ch 8	The study of salvation; how God rescues us.
Justification	Ch 8	God declaring us "righteous" the moment we believe.
Sanctification	Ch 10	The process of becoming more holy over time.
Ecclesiology	Ch 9	The study of the Church; the Body of Christ.
Angelology	Ch 11	The study of angels, demons, and spiritual warfare.
Eschatology	Ch 12	The study of the end times and the return of Jesus.

EXTRA WORKBOOK SECTION
THE DEEP DIVE

You have finished the book. You have read the chapters, learned the big words, and hopefully started to see God in a bigger way. But reading about swimming is not the same as jumping into the ocean. Up until now, we have been wading in the shallow end—getting comfortable with the water, learning the strokes, and understanding the basics. Now, it is time to go deeper.

This **Extra Workbook Section** is designed to be your companion for the next few months. It is not something you rush through in a weekend. It is a toolkit. Think of it like a gym membership for your soul. You don't go to the gym once for 12 hours and expect to be fit; you go for 45 minutes, three times a week, for a year. That is how spiritual growth happens.

This section is divided into five parts:

1. **Bible Study Methods:** Tools to help you feed yourself from God's Word.
2. **Theology in Culture:** How to keep your faith when the world is loud.
3. **Apologetics Bootcamp:** How to defend what you believe.
4. **Prayer & Fasting:** How to connect with God's heart.
5. **Service & Mission:** How to be the hands and feet of Jesus.

Grab a pen, a Bible, and maybe a cup of coffee. Let's get to work.

Part 1: The "Deep Dive" Bible Study Methods

Many teens struggle with reading the Bible because they don't know *how* to read it. They open it up, read a random verse, get confused, and close it. This section will teach you four specific methods to study Scripture. These are tools you can use for the rest of your life.

Method 1: The S.O.A.P. Method

This is the classic, go-to method for daily devotions. It is simple enough to do in 15 minutes but deep enough to change your day.

- **S - Scripture:** Write out the verse or passage you are studying. Writing it helps you slow down and see details you might miss just by reading.
- **O - Observation:** What do you see? Who is talking? What is the context? Are there any repeating words? What is the mood of the passage? (Don't interpret yet; just observe).
- **A - Application:** How does this apply to me *today*? Is there a command to obey? A sin to avoid? A promise to claim? Be specific.
- **P - Prayer:** Write a short prayer back to God based on what you just read.

Guided Exercise: Let's practice with **Psalm 1:1-3**. *"Blessed is the man who walks not in the counsel of the wicked, nor stands in the way of sinners, nor sits in the seat of scoffers; but his delight is in the law of the Lord, and on his law he meditates day and night. He is like a tree planted by streams of water that yields its fruit in its season, and its leaf does not wither. In all that he does, he prospers."*

Your Turn:

- **Scripture:** (Copy the verses above in your own handwriting here):

- **Observation:** (List 3 things you notice. Example: The progression of "walk, stand, sit.")

  1. ____

  2. ____

  3. ____

- **Application:** (How does the "counsel of the wicked" look in your school? Who are you listening to?)

- **Prayer:** (Ask God to help you delight in His law).

Method 2: The Character Study

The Bible is full of flawed people used by a perfect God. Studying their lives helps us see how God interacts with humans. **The Steps:**

1. **Pick a Person:** (e.g., Peter, Ruth, David, Esther).

2. **Gather the References:** Use a concordance or online Bible tool to find where they appear.

3. **Ask the "Big Three" Questions:**
    - What were their strengths?
    - What were their weaknesses/sins?
    - What did they learn about God?

Guided Exercise: The Apostle Peter

- **Passages to Read:** Luke 5:1-11 (The Call), Matthew 14:28-31 (Walking on Water), Matthew 26:69-75 (The Denial), John 21:15-19 (The Restoration).

- **Strengths:** (e.g., Boldness, willingness to step out of the boat).

- **Weaknesses:** (e.g., Fear of man, speaking without thinking).

- **The Lesson:** How did Jesus treat Peter after he messed up? What does this tell you about how Jesus treats you?

Method 3: The Verse Mapping

This is for the visual learners. Verse mapping involves breaking a verse down diagrammatically. You circle key words, draw lines to connect thoughts, and look up definitions of original Greek or Hebrew words.

Guided Exercise: Romans 12:2 *"Do not be conformed to this world, but be transformed by the renewal of your mind, that by testing you may discern what is the will of God, what is good and acceptable and perfect."*

1. **Circle "Conformed":** Look up the definition. (It means "poured into a mold").

   Reflection: What "molds" is the world trying to pour you into right now? (e.g., The mold of popularity, the mold of greed).

   ----

2. **Box "Transformed":** The Greek word is *metamorphoo* (where we get "metamorphosis").

   Reflection: How is a butterfly different from a caterpillar? How should a Christian be different from their old self?

   ----

3. **Underline "Renewal of your mind":**

   Reflection: What are you feeding your mind? (TikTok, Netflix, Scripture?). Garbage in, garbage out.

Method 4: The Keyword Trace

Sometimes a single word can unlock a huge theological truth. **The Word:** *Shalom* (Peace).

1. **Old Testament Meaning:** It doesn't just mean "no war." It means wholeness, completeness, everything working as it should.

2. **New Testament Fulfillment:** Jesus is the "Prince of Peace."

3. **Your Study:** Find 3 verses that use the word "Peace."
   - Verse 1: ____
   - Verse 2: ____
   - Verse 3: ____
   - **Synthesis:** Based on these verses, is peace a feeling or a fact? _____________________________________

We do not live in a bubble. We live in a world that is constantly preaching a sermon to us. Every movie, every song, and every advertisement is telling you what the "good life" is. Theology helps you put on "Jesus Glasses" so you can see the lies and find the truth.

Challenge 1: The Playlist Audit

Music is powerful because it bypasses our logic and goes straight to our emotions. **The Task:** Pick the top 3 songs on your current "On Repeat" playlist. **The Analysis:**

1. **Song Title:**

   ----

2. **The Message:** What is the singer saying will make them happy? (Money, a relationship, **revenge**, partying).

   ----

3. **The Theology Check:** Compare that message to Scripture.
   - *Song says:* "I need you to complete me."
   - *Bible says:* "You are complete in Christ" (Colossians 2:10).
   - *Verdict:* Is this song telling the truth, a lie, or a half-truth?

Challenge 2: The Movie Watch-Along

Next time you watch a movie, don't just consume it; critique it. **The Movie:**

The Questions:

1. **The Villain:** Why is the bad guy bad? usually, it's because they want power, or they are hurt. How does this reflect the biblical idea of sin?

   ----

2. **The Hero:** Does the hero sacrifice themselves? Almost every great movie has a "Christ-figure"—someone who gives up their life for others. Why do you think human beings love that story so much?

----

3. **The Redemption:** How is the problem solved? Is it through violence, forgiveness, or love?

Challenge 3: The Social Media Detox

Social media is designed to make you compare your "behind-the-scenes" with everyone else's "highlight reel." **The Audit:** Go through your "Following" list on Instagram or TikTok.

1. **Identify:** Find 3 accounts that consistently make you feel jealous, angry, or lustful.

   o *Account 1:* ____________________________________
   o *Account 2:* ____________________________________
   o *Account 3:* ____________________________________

2. **The Action:** Mute or Unfollow them for 30 days.

3. **The Replacement:** Find 3 accounts that encourage your faith or teach you something valuable.

   o *Account 1:* ____________________________________
   o *Account 2:* ____________________________________
   o *Account 3:* ____________________________________

Challenge 4: The News Prayer Cycle

Instead of getting anxious about the headlines, turn them into prayer requests. **Current Event:**

- **Who is hurting?** Pray for their comfort.

- **Who is leading?** Pray for wisdom for the politicians/leaders involved.

____

____

- **Where is the Church?** Pray for the Christians in that area to be a light.

____

____

Part 3: The "Apologetics" Bootcamp

"Apologetics" comes from the Greek word *apologia*, which means "to give a defense." 1 Peter 3:15 says, "Always be prepared to make a defense to anyone who asks you for a reason for the hope that is in you."

You will face questions. Here is how to answer three of the biggest ones.

Unit 1: Does God Exist?

The Argument from Design (Teleological Argument): Imagine you are walking on a beach and find a smartphone in the sand. You pick it up, turn it on, and see it has apps, a camera, and a battery. Would you assume that the sand and the waves just randomly crashed together for millions of years and accidentally formed the phone? No. You would assume a designer made it. The universe is far more complex than a smartphone. The distance of the earth from the sun, the tilt of the axis, the complexity of the human eye, all of these are "fine-tuned" for life.

- **The Defense:** "The universe has a complex design. A design requires a Designer. Therefore, the universe has a Designer."

The Argument from Morality: Every culture in history knows that certain things (like murdering a child for fun) are wrong. Where does this "moral law" come from? If we are just accidents of evolution, "wrong" is just a matter of opinion. But we feel deep down that "wrong" is real.

- **The Defense:** "If there is a Moral Law, there must be a Moral Lawgiver."

Unit 2: Why is there Evil?

This is the hardest question. "If God is all-good and all-powerful, why do bad things happen?" **The Free Will Defense:** God wanted to create a world where love was possible. For love to be real, it must be free. You cannot force a robot to love you. But if you give creatures the freedom to love, you also give them the freedom *not* to love, to hate, to kill, and to sin. Evil is the result of humans misusing their freedom. **The "Soul-Making" Theodicy:** God is more interested in your character than your comfort. Often, we grow the most during hard times. A gym trainer makes you lift heavy weights not because he hates you, but because he wants you to be strong. God can use suffering to make us more like Jesus.

- **The Defense:** "God has not removed evil yet, but He has defeated it at the cross, and one day He will remove it forever."

Unit 3: Is the Bible Reliable?

"Isn't the Bible just a game of telephone? Hasn't it been changed over thousands of years?" **The Manuscript Evidence:** We have more ancient copies of the New Testament than any other book in history.

- *Caesar's Gallic Wars:* written 50 BC, earliest copy 900 AD (Gap: 950 years). Copies: 10.

- *New Testament:* written 50-90 AD, earliest fragments 120 AD (Gap: 30-70 years). Copies: Over 5,800 in Greek alone. **The Archaeological Evidence:** Time and again, archaeology confirms the Bible. We have found the Pool of Siloam, the Pilate Stone, and the walls of Jericho.

- **The Defense:** "The Bible is the best-attested document of ancient history. We can trust that what we have today is what was written then."

Roleplay: The Skeptical Friend Imagine your friend Sam says: *"I believe in science, not fairy tales. Religion is just a crutch for weak people."*

- **How would you respond with gentleness and respect?** (Hint: Ask questions. "What do you mean by 'crutch'?" "Do you think science can answer questions about love or purpose?")

Prayer is the breath of the soul. If you stop breathing, you die. If you stop praying, your faith withers.

Section 1: The A.C.T.S. Model

If you get stuck and don't know what to say, use this acronym.

- **A - Adoration:** Praising God for who He is. "God, You are..."
- **C - Confession:** Admitting where you messed up. "God, I am sorry for..."
- **T - Thanksgiving:** Thanking God for what He has done. "God, thank You for..."
- **S - Supplication:** Asking God for what you need. "God, please help..."

Practice: Write a 4-sentence prayer using ACTS right now.

1. (A) ____
2. (C) ____
3. (T) ____
4. (S) ____

Section 2: Listening Prayer

We often treat prayer like a voicemail where we leave a message and hang up. But it is a conversation. **The Exercise:** Set a timer for 3 minutes. Close your eyes. Do not talk. Just sit in silence and ask, "God, do you want to say anything to me?"

- *Note:* God usually speaks through a quiet thought, a Bible verse popping into your head, or a sense of peace. He will never contradict His Bible.
- **What came to mind during the silence?**

____

____

____

Section 3: A Teen's Guide to Fasting

Fasting is voluntarily giving up something good for a spiritual purpose. It tells your body, "I need God more than I need this." **What can you fast from?**

- **Food:** (Skip one meal, like lunch. Note: If you have any history of eating disorders, talk to a doctor or parent first and fast from something else).
- **Technology:** (No Instagram for 24 hours).
- **Entertainment:** (No video games or Netflix for a weekend).

The Purpose: Every time your stomach growls or you reach for your phone, use that as a reminder to pray. **Your Plan:**

- I will fast from:

____

- For this long:

____

- My spiritual goal is:

____

Section 4: The 7-Day Prayer Challenge

Commit to praying for these specific things for the next week.

- **Day 1:** Your Family (Unity, health, salvation).
- **Day 2:** Your School (For bullying to stop, for teachers).
- **Day 3:** Your Pastors/Leaders (For strength, protection from temptation).
- **Day 4:** The Unsaved (List 3 friends who don't know Jesus).
- **Day 5:** The Global Church (Christians being persecuted in other countries).
- **Day 6:** Your Future (Your future spouse, career, calling).
- **Day 7:** Yourself (For purity, wisdom, and courage).

Part 5: The "Service & Mission" Project Planner

Christianity is not a spectator sport. You have a jersey, and you are on the field.

Step 1: Discover Your Gifts

Read the list below and circle the ones that resonate with you.

- **Serving:** You see a mess and clean it up. You like helping behind the scenes.
- **Teaching:** You like explaining things so people understand.

- **Encouragement:** You love cheering people up and writing notes.
- **Giving:** You love being generous with your money or stuff.
- **Leadership:** People naturally follow you when you have an idea.
- **Mercy:** You feel deep sadness for people who are hurting or lonely.
- **Hospitality:** You love making people feel welcome and comfortable.

My Top 2 Gifts seem to be:

1. ____
2. ____

Step 2: Map Your Neighborhood

Who is around you?

- **The Elderly Neighbor:** Does their lawn need mowing? Do they need someone to talk to?
- **The Single Mom:** Could she use a free babysitter for a night?
- **The "Weird" Kid at School:** Do they sit alone at lunch?
- **The Teacher:** Do they look stressed? Could you write them a thank-you note?

One specific need I see right now is:

____

____

Step 3: The "Micro-Mission" Ideas

You don't need to go to Africa to be a missionary. You can start in your kitchen. **Pick one of these to do THIS WEEK:**

- [ ] Bake cookies for a neighbor and leave a note saying, "God loves you and so do I."
- [ ] Text 3 friends and ask, "How can I pray for you today?"
- [ ] Donate your old clothes to a shelter.
- [ ] Ask your parents, "What is one chore you hate doing?" and do it for them without being asked.

Step 4: Sharing the Gospel

If someone asked you, "How do I become a Christian?" would you know what to say? Here are two simple methods. Learn one of them.

Method A: The Roman Road Using verses from the book of Romans to explain salvation.

1. **The Problem:** Romans 3:23 ("All have sinned...").
2. **The Consequence:** Romans 6:23 ("The wages of sin is death...").
3. **The Solution:** Romans 5:8 ("But God shows his love for us in that while we were still sinners, Christ died for us").
4. **The Response:** Romans 10:9 ("If you confess... and believe... you will be saved").

Method B: The Three Circles

1. **Circle 1: God's Design.** God made a perfect world full of love.
2. **The Arrow:** Sin took us away from God's design.
3. **Circle 2: Brokenness.** We are now in a broken world (pain, death). We try to fix it with money or popularity (squiggly lines), but they just snap back.
4. **Circle 3: The Gospel.** Jesus came into our brokenness, died, and rose again.
5. **The Response:** If we turn (repent) and believe, we are restored to God's Design.

Practice: Write out the Roman Road verses on an index card and keep it in your wallet/backpack.

EXTRA WORKBOOK SECTION
TEAMWORK

Welcome to the Teamwork Section. If you are reading this, it means you have decided to do something radical. In a world that prizes independence, "self-made" success, and digital isolation, you have chosen to walk the road of faith with others.

Christianity was never designed to be a solo sport. When Jesus started His ministry, the very first thing He did was build a small group. He didn't write a book; He called twelve disciples. He knew that for the truth to survive and for hearts to change, people needed *koinonia*—the Greek word for deep, shared life.

There is a dangerous myth in modern culture called the "Lone Wolf" Christian. This is the person who says, "I love Jesus, but I don't need the church. I can worship God on a hike or in my bedroom just fine." While it is true that you can worship God anywhere, it is impossible to grow into the full image of Christ by yourself. You cannot learn patience without someone to annoy you. You cannot learn forgiveness without someone to hurt you. You cannot learn to serve without someone who has needs.

This workbook section is designed for a group of 3 to 12 friends. You can do this as a youth small group, a lunch club at school, or just a few friends hanging out in a living room. It is a **5-Week Journey** that will take the theology you learned in the main book and force you to live it out in community.

Ground Rules for the Journey:

1. **Commitment:** If you are in, be in. Show up for all 5 weeks.
2. **Confidentiality:** What is said in the room stays in the room. This is the "Vegas Rule" of small groups. If people don't feel safe, they won't be real.
3. **Honesty:** Leave the masks at the door. You don't have to impress anyone here. We are all messy, and we are all in need of grace.
4. **Bible-Centered:** Our opinions are interesting, but God's Word is authoritative. We will always come back to the Text.

How to Use This Section:

- **Designate a Facilitator:** This doesn't have to be a teacher or an adult. It's just someone to read the questions and keep the conversation moving.
- **Bring Supplies:** You will need Bibles, journals, pens, and occasionally some paper or a whiteboard.
- **Pray First:** Never start a session without asking the Holy Spirit to be present.

Week 1: The Foundation (Unmasking)

Objective: To move from shallow friendship to spiritual brotherhood/sisterhood by sharing our stories and establishing a "Covenant of Grace."

Part 1: The Setup (15 Minutes)

Facilitator Read: "We are starting Week 1. The goal today is simple: we want to know who we actually are. Most of us wear masks at school. We have a 'Cool Mask,' a 'Smart Mask,' or a 'Funny Mask.' We wear them to protect ourselves because we are afraid that if people saw our real struggles, they wouldn't like us. But the Gospel says we are fully known by God and still fully loved. That gives us the courage to drop the masks with each other."

Icebreaker: "The Photo Scroll"

- Everyone take out your phone.
- Scroll back to a photo from at least 1 year ago.
- Show the group and explain: *What was happening in this photo? What is one thing you loved about that time, and one thing that was hard about that time that the camera didn't capture?*

Part 2: The Theology of "One Another" (20 Minutes)

Bible Study: Have someone read **Romans 12:3-13** aloud.

Discussion Questions:

1. **Verse 5** says we are "individually members one of another." This is a weird phrase. It suggests we belong to each other, like a hand belongs to an arm.
   - *Question:* Do you usually feel like you "belong" to the other Christians in your life? Why or why not?

2. **Verse 9** says, "Let love be genuine." The Greek word here is *anypokritos*, which means "without a mask" or "not acting."
   - *Question:* What does "fake love" look like in a friend group? What does "genuine love" look like?
3. **Verse 10** says, "Outdo one another in showing honor."
   - *Question:* Imagine a competition where everyone is trying to honor the other person more. How would that change the vibe of your school or group?

Part 3: The Activity - "Life Maps" (45 Minutes)

Materials Needed: Large sheets of paper and markers for everyone.

Instructions: You are going to draw a "Map" of your life journey so far. This isn't an art contest; it's a way to visualize your story.

1. **The Start:** Draw a symbol for where you were born or your early family life.
2. **The Highs:** Draw "Mountains" for the best moments (e.g., winning a championship, a great vacation, getting saved).
3. **The Lows:** Draw "Valleys" for the hardest moments (e.g., parents divorcing, moving schools, a health struggle, a season of depression).
4. **The Turns:** Draw "Road Signs" for moments where your life changed direction (e.g., meeting a certain friend, a youth camp, a bad choice).
5. **The Current Location:** Draw a symbol for where you are right now with God (e.g., a desert, a garden, a battlefield, a fog).

Sharing: Give everyone 10-15 minutes to draw. Then, go around the circle. Each person has 3-5 minutes to explain their map.

- *Crucial Rule:* While someone is sharing, no one interrupts. You just listen. At the end, simply say, "Thank you for sharing," or "I appreciate your honesty."

Reflection:

- Did you learn something new about someone you thought you knew well?
- Did you see any common themes in the "Valleys" of the group?

Part 4: The Covenant (10 Minutes)

Facilitator Read: "Now that we have shared our stories, we need to agree on how we will treat each other. A 'Covenant' is a serious promise. It is heavier than a contract."

The Group Covenant: Read these aloud together. If everyone agrees, sign a piece of paper with these points written on it.

- **I Promise Confidentiality:** I will not gossip about what is shared here.
- **I Promise Grace:** I will not judge you for your struggles, but point you to Jesus.
- **I Promise Truth:** I will speak the truth in love, even when it is hard.
- **I Promise Prayer:** I will pray for this group during the week.

Part 5: Closing Prayer (5 Minutes)

Don't just have one person pray. Do "Popcorn Prayer."

- Everyone pick one person on their right.
- Pray one sentence for that person based on the "Life Map" they shared.
- (Example: "Lord, please help Sarah in the 'valley' she is in right now.")

Homework for Week 2: Read **Colossians 3:1-17** every day this week. Just read it. Don't study it yet. Just let it soak in.

Week 2: The Study (Digging Deeps)

Objective: To learn how to feed ourselves from the Bible *together* using the Inductive Bible Study Method, moving from passive listening to active discovery.

Part 1: The Warm-Up (10 Minutes)

Check-In:

- How was your week?
- Did anyone actually read Colossians 3? Be honest!
- *Theology Recap:* Who remembers what **Sanctification** means? (Answer: The process of becoming holy/more like Jesus). Today, we are going to look at the "Instruction Manual" for Sanctification.

Part 2: The Method - Observation (20 Minutes)

Facilitator Note: "We are going to be detectives today. We are looking at **Colossians 3:1-17**. We will use three steps: Observation (What does it say?), Interpretation (What does it mean?), and Application (What do I do?)."

Read Colossians 3:1-17 Aloud. (Ideally, have different people read 3 verses each).

Group Exercise: The Whiteboard Deconstruction (If you don't have a whiteboard, use a big piece of paper in the middle of the room).

Ask the group to shout out "Observations." Write them down.

- *Look for Contrasts:* What is being compared? (e.g., "Things above" vs. "Things on earth").

- *Look for Commands:* What are we told to do? (e.g., "Seek," "Set your minds," "Put to death").

- *Look for Lists:* There are two lists in this passage—a "Kill List" (verses 5-9) and a "Wear List" (verses 12-14). Let's list them out side-by-side.

The Lists (Write these out):

- **Put to Death (The Old Self):** Evil desire, covetousness, anger, wrath, malice, slander, obscene talk, lying.

- **Put On (The New Self):** Compassionate hearts, kindness, humility, meekness, patience, bearing with one another, forgiveness, love, peace, thankfulness.

Part 3: The Deep Dive - Interpretation (30 Minutes)

Discussion Questions:

1. **The "Clothing" Metaphor:** Paul uses the language of changing clothes ("put off" and "put on").

    - *Question:* Why is this a good picture of the Christian life? Can you wear "clean clothes" (kindness) over "dirty clothes" (anger)? No, you have to take the old off first.

    - *Theology Check:* This relates to **Justification** vs. **Sanctification**. We *are* new creations (Justification), but we have to *choose* to dress like it (Sanctification).

2. **The "Kill" List:** Look at verse 5. It says "Put to death." It doesn't say "manage" or "suppress."

    o *Question:* Why does the Bible use such violent language for sin? What happens if you try to "tame" a sin like greed or lust instead of killing it?

    o *Discussion:* Which of the sins in the "Put to Death" list do you think is most accepted in high school culture today? (e.g., Slander/Gossip is often seen as normal).

3. **The "Super-Glue" of Love:** Verse 14 says, "And above all these put on love, which binds everything together in perfect harmony."

    o *Question:* Imagine you have patience and humility but no love. What does that look like? (Maybe you are just acting polite but secretly resentful). Why is love the "binder"?

Part 4: The Application Grid (20 Minutes)

Activity: Give everyone a piece of paper. Draw a grid with 4 squares. Label them:

1. **Home/Family**
2. **School/Work**
3. **Friends/Group**
4. **Enemies/Annoying People**

Instructions: Pick **ONE** quality from the "Put On" list (Compassion, Kindness, Humility, Meekness, Patience, Forgiveness). Write that quality in the middle of the page. Now, write one specific action you can do in each square to show that quality this week.

- *Example: Patience.*

    o *Home:* I will not snap at my mom when she asks about homework.

    o *School:* I will wait for the slow walker in the hallway without sighing.

    o *Friends:* I will listen to [Name]'s story without interrupting.

    o *Enemies:* I will pray for the person who bullied me instead of roasting them.

Share: Ask for volunteers to share one of their application points.

Part 5: Worship & Word (10 Minutes)

Verse 16 says, "Let the word of Christ dwell in you richly... singing psalms and hymns and spiritual songs."

- If your group is musical, sing a song together (acapella or with a guitar).
- If not, play a worship song on a speaker.
- *Challenge:* Don't just listen. Sing. Make it a declaration that you are "Putting On" the new self.

Homework for Week 3: Identify one "Stronghold" or persistent struggle in your life (e.g., anxiety, lust, anger, procrastination). Come ready to talk about it next week (as much as you feel safe).

Week 3: The Battle (Accountability)

Objective: To recognize the reality of spiritual warfare and to set up a system of accountability where we fight *for* each other, not just *with* each other.

Part 1: The War Room Context (10 Minutes)

Facilitator Read: "Welcome to the Bunker. Last week we looked at the clothes we need to wear. Today we look at the armor. We learned in the **Angelology** chapter that we have an enemy. Satan loves to isolate Christians. He knows that a zebra separated from the herd is easy prey. He wants you to keep your struggles secret. He whispers, 'If they knew the truth about you, they would reject you.' Today, we prove him wrong."

Theology Check: Hamartiology (Sin) & **Spiritual Warfare**.

- Sin thrives in the dark.
- Confession brings it into the light.
- James 5:16 says, "Confess your sins to one another and pray for one another, *that you may be healed*." Note: We confess to God for *forgiveness*, but we confess to each other for *healing*.

Part 2: The "Hot Seat" of Grace (40 Minutes)

Disclaimer: This activity requires maturity. The goal is encouragement, not interrogation.

The Concept: We are going to go around the circle. One person is in the "Hot Seat." They will answer two questions:

1. **Where are you winning right now?** (Where do you see God working? What are you proud of?)

2. **Where are you fighting right now?** (What is the struggle you identified for homework? Where are you weak?)

The Rules for the Listeners:

- **No Fixing:** Do not say, "Oh, have you tried this app?" or "You should just read more." Just listen.

- **No Shaming:** Do not gasp or look shocked.

- **Affirmation:** After they share, the group must speak truth over them. (e.g., "I see God's grace in you," or "You are brave for sharing that.")

The Practice: Spend about 5-7 minutes per person. If the group is large (over 8), split into two smaller groups for this.

- *Example Share:* "I am winning in my prayer life; I've prayed every morning. But I am fighting with lust. I keep looking at things I shouldn't on my phone late at night."

- *Example Response:* "Thank you for trusting us. We are with you. You are not defined by that struggle. You are a child of God."

Part 3: The Shield Wall (20 Minutes)

Activity: In ancient Rome, soldiers used a formation called the *testudo* (tortoise). They would lock their shields together. If one soldier dropped his shield, the guy next to him would get hit. We need to lock shields.

Partner Up: Break into pairs (same gender is usually best for this). This is your **"Shield Partner"** for the rest of the month. Exchange phone numbers if you don't have them.

The Assignment: You must text your Shield Partner at least **three times** this week.

- **Text 1 (Check-in):** "How is the battle today?"

- **Text 2 (Scripture):** Send a verse that encourages them.

- **Text 3 (Prayer):** "How can I pray for you right now?"

Discuss in Pairs:

- What is the best time of day to check in?

- What is your "Code Red"? (e.g., If I am really tempted, can I text you "Code Red" and you just pray immediately?)

Part 4: Prayer focus - The Armor (15 Minutes)

Corporate Prayer: Come back together as a big group. We are going to pray through **Ephesians 6:10-18** for the person on our left.

- *Leader:* "Lord, we equip [Name] with the Belt of Truth."
- *Group:* "Let them know what is real and reject the lies."
- *Leader:* "We equip [Name] with the Breastplate of Righteousness."
- *Group:* "Guard their heart and emotions."
- *Leader:* "We equip [Name] with the Shoes of Peace."
- *Group:* "Let them bring peace to their school."
- *Leader:* "We equip [Name] with the Shield of Faith."
- *Group:* "Extinguish every flaming arrow of doubt."
- *Leader:* "We equip [Name] with the Helmet of Salvation."
- *Group:* "Protect their mind and thoughts."
- *Leader:* "We give [Name] the Sword of the Spirit."
- *Group:* "Let Your Word be in their mouth."

Part 5: Conclusion (5 Minutes)

Facilitator Read: "You are no longer fighting alone. When you are tempted this week, remember: there is a Shield Partner and a whole room of people standing with you. Don't drop your shield."

Homework for Week 4: Think of **three people** in your life who do not know Jesus. Write their names down on a card and bring it next week.

Week 4: The Outward Look (The Search Party)

Objective: To turn our focus outward, equipping the team for evangelism and service. We move from the "Bunker" to the "Field."

Part 1: The Huddle (10 Minutes)

Theology Check: Soteriology (Salvation) & **Missiology** (Mission).

- **Soteriology** teaches us that salvation is a free gift of grace.
- **Missiology** teaches us that we are the delivery drivers of that gift.

- **Analogy:** Imagine you found the cure for cancer, but you kept it in your basement while your neighbors were dying. That would be criminal. We have the cure for death (the Gospel). We must share it.

Reflect:

- Why is sharing our faith so scary? (Fear of rejection, not knowing answers, looking weird).

- How does doing it as a *team* make it easier?

Part 2: The Apologetics Dojo (30 Minutes)

Facilitator Note: "We are going to spar. We need to practice answering hard questions so we don't freeze up when they happen in real life."

Roleplay Activity: Split into groups of 3.

- **Person A:** The Skeptic (Ask a tough question).

- **Person B:** The Christian (Answer with gentleness and respect).

- **Person C:** The Coach (Watch and give feedback).

Scenario 1: The "Good Person" Argument

- *Skeptic:* "I don't need Jesus. I'm a good person. I don't kill anyone. If God is real, He'll let me into heaven because I'm nice."

- *Christian Goal:* Explain that God's standard is perfection, not just "niceness," and that's why we need a Savior (Romans 3:23).

- *Coach:* Did they get defensive? Did they use the Bible?

Scenario 2: The "Intolerant" Argument

- *Skeptic:* "Christians are so judgmental. You think you're the only ones who are right. That's arrogant."

- *Christian Goal:* Explain that truth isn't about arrogance; it's about reality. (e.g., "If a doctor tells you have an illness, is he arrogant, or is he trying to help you?"). Focus on Jesus saying "I am the Way" (John 14:6).

Scenario 3: The "Suffering" Argument

- *Skeptic:* "If God loves us, why did my grandma die of cancer?"

- *Christian Goal:* Don't try to solve the mystery of evil. Show empathy. "I am so sorry about your grandma. The Bible actually says death is an enemy. Jesus hates death too—He wept at a tomb. He came to defeat it."

Switch Roles: Rotate so everyone gets a turn being the Christian.

Part 3: The "Three Circles" Drill (20 Minutes)

Review: Refer back to the "Three Circles" method from the Extra Workbook Section (Brokenness -> God's Design -> Gospel).

Practice: Get a partner. Take 2 minutes each to explain the Gospel to each other using the Three Circles. Use a piece of paper and draw it while you talk.

- *Tip:* Keep it simple. Don't use big "Christianese" words like *Propitiation* or *Sanctification* when talking to a non-believer. Use words like *Broken, Restored, Trust*.

Part 4: The Neighborhood Watch (20 Minutes)

The Name Cards: Take out the cards with the 3 names you wrote down for homework. Place them all in the center of the room (or on a table).

The Prayer Circle: Gather around the names. We are going to pray for them "Harvest Style."

- Pray that God would soften their hearts (The Soil).
- Pray for an opportunity to speak to them this week (The Open Door).
- Pray for courage to invite them to church/youth group (The Invitation).

The Service Project Brainstorm: As a team, you need to do one outward act together this month.

- *Brainstorm ideas:*
  - Buy 20 burgers and hand them out to homeless people downtown.
  - Go to a local park and pick up trash for an hour.
  - Write "Thank You" cards for the school janitors and cafeteria staff and deliver them with donuts.
  - Offer to do yard work for an elderly neighbor of one of the group members.

Decision: Vote on one project. Set a date. Assign roles (Who buys supplies? Who drives? Who brings the speaker for music?).

Part 5: Closing (10 Minutes)

Facilitator Read: "We are a search party. This week, keep your eyes open. Look for the people on your cards. Look for the lonely. If you see an opportunity, take it. And text your Shield Partner if you get nervous!"

Homework for Week 5: Bring an object that represents your hope for the future (it can be anything—a picture, a tool, a souvenir). Also, write a short letter to *each* person in the group (just 1-2 sentences of encouragement).

Week 5: The Future (The Launchpad)

Objective: To solidify the bonds formed, celebrate growth, and commission the group to live with an eternal perspective.

Part 1: The Theology of Hope (15 Minutes)

Theology Check: Eschatology (The End Times/Future).

- Eschatology isn't just about the end of the world; it's about the goal of history.
- We are moving toward a Wedding Feast (Revelation 19).
- We are moving toward a New Earth where righteousness dwells.
- Because we know the end of the story, we can endure the messy middle chapters.

Discussion:

- Show the "Object of Hope" you brought. Explain why you picked it.
- *Question:* How does knowing that Jesus wins in the end help you when you have a bad day at school?

Part 2: The "Speak Life" Ceremony (40 Minutes)

The Concept: Proverbs 18:21 says, "Death and life are in the power of the tongue." We usually hear a lot of death (criticism, sarcasm, insults). Today, we speak life.

The Activity: One person sits in the middle (or focus on one person at a time in the circle). Everyone else reads the short note/letter they wrote for that person.

- *Specific Encouragement:* Don't just say "You're nice." Say, "I see the gift of leadership in you," or "Your joy makes our group better," or "I admire how you stood up for your faith."
- *Prophetic Encouragement:* "I believe God is going to use you to..."

The Recipient: The person receiving the encouragement cannot deflect it. They cannot say, "Oh, no, I'm not that great." They must simply say, "Thank you, I receive that."

Repeat: Go around until everyone has been encouraged. This will take time, and it will likely be emotional. Let it be. This is *koinonia*.

Part 3: The Covenant Meal (Communion) (20 Minutes)

Facilitator Note: *Check with your church leadership/parents about leading Communion. If you are not comfortable or authorized to do formal Communion, call this a "Covenant Meal" and share food together with spiritual intent.*

The Setup: Have bread/crackers and juice/grapes ready.

The Reading: Read **1 Corinthians 11:23-26**.

The Reflection: Before eating, take a moment of silence.

- Look back at the last 5 weeks.
- Thank Jesus that *He* is the one who made this community possible. His body was broken so we could be the "Body of Christ." His blood was shed to sign the New Covenant.

The Partaking: Serve one another. Pass the bread and juice around.

- As you pass it, say: "The Body of Christ, broken for you." / "The Blood of Christ, shed for you."

The Feast: After the solemn moment, eat! If you brought snacks or a meal (pizza, etc.), transition into hanging out and eating together. The early church always connected Communion with a "Love Feast" (a full meal).

Part 4: The "Time Capsule" (10 Minutes)

Activity: Take a piece of paper. Write a letter to your "Future Self" (Open in 1 Year).

- What did you learn in this study?
- What do you want to remember about God?

- What are you praying for your future self to be doing?
- Who are you praying for?

Seal it: Put it in an envelope. Write the date "Open [Date] Next Year." Give all the envelopes to the Facilitator (or a responsible person) to keep safe, or have everyone keep their own in their Bible.

Part 5: The Final Commissioning (5 Minutes)

Facilitator Read: "We are done with the workbook, but we are not done with the work. The huddle breaks, and the play begins.

- Keep your Covenants.
- Keep texting your Shield Partners.
- Keep looking for the lost.
- Keep your eyes on the King."

The Huddle Break: Everyone stand up. Put hands in the middle. Facilitator prays a loud prayer of sending. **"1, 2, 3... GO!"**

Appendix: Resources for the Leader

How to Handle "Awkward Silence"

When you ask a question and no one answers, **wait**. Count to 10 in your head. People are thinking. If the silence goes too long, rephrase the question. "Let me ask it a different way..." Don't answer your own question.

How to Handle the "Over-Talker"

If one person dominates the conversation:

- Affirm them: "Thanks, [Name], that's a great point."
- Pivot: "I'd love to hear from someone who hasn't shared yet. Sarah? Mike?"
- Talk privately: If it continues, pull them aside gently after the meeting. "Hey, I love your passion, but I want to make sure we leave space for the quiet ones to share."

How to Handle "Heavy" Confessions

If someone confesses something serious (self-harm, abuse, suicidal thoughts, serious addiction):

1. **Stay Calm.** Don't freak out.
2. **Thank them.** "Thank you for being brave enough to share that."

3. **Do not keep it a secret.** If it involves safety (abuse or suicide), you *must* tell a trusted adult (Youth Pastor, Parent, Counselor). Remind them of the "Limits of Confidentiality" (we keep secrets unless you are hurting yourself or others are hurting you).

4. **Pray immediately.**

Spotify Playlist Recommendations for Week 2 & 5

- *Elevation Worship* - "Available"
- *Hillsong United* - "Good Grace"
- *Phil Wickham* - "Battle Belongs"
- *Maverick City Music* - "Jireh"
- *Citizens* - "In Tenderness"

Snack Ideas

- *Week 1:* Popcorn (easy, sharable).
- *Week 2:* Sour Patch Kids (sweet and sour, like the "Put Off/Put On" list).
- *Week 3:* Warheads or something intense (for the "Battle").
- *Week 4:* Donuts (round, like the "3 Circles").
- *Week 5:* Pizza party or a Potluck.

HERE'S ANOTHER BOOK BY JAMES NORTHWELL
THAT YOU MIGHT LIKE

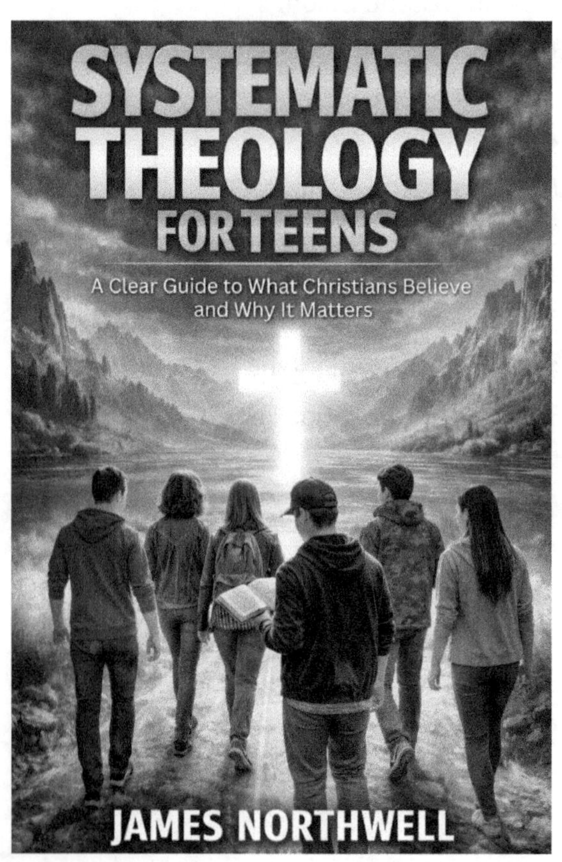